Developing Equitable Education Systems

Despite consistent improvements in school systems over recent years, there are still too many children who miss out. For whatever reason, schooling does not seem to be working for these young people. Recent OECD reports indicate that the incidence of this problem is much higher among disadvantaged groups. But it is not only children from disadvantaged backgrounds attending hard-pressed urban schools that the system is failing – even in the most successful schools there are often groups of learners whose experience of schooling is less than equitable.

As a result of their close involvement with a group of English schools serving a predominantly working-class community over five years, the authors of this book – a team of researchers with international experience and reputations – offer an analysis of how such marginalisation within schools can arise, and provide suggestions for responding to this crucial policy agenda. Specifically, they propose a teacher-led inquiry strategy that has proved to be effective in moving forward thinking and practice within individual schools. However, their research has also shown that its use as a strategy for system change remains problematic within a policy context that emphasises competition and choice. Learning from this experience, the authors analyse the factors that inhibit the collaborative approach needed to reduce inequities that exist between the schools, in order to formulate proposals that can move the system as a whole towards more equitable provision.

Developing Equitable Education Systems focuses on the way teachers' sense of 'fairness' can become a powerful starting point, helping individual schools to inquire into and develop their own practice and provision. In so doing, the book provides practical suggestions for practitioners about ways of working that can create a greater sense of equity within particular school contexts. It also highlights the barriers to a wider strategy for reducing system inequities that reside in local and national policies and traditions.

As government policies in many countries move to extend the diversity of educational provision – for example, through the introduction of charter schools in the USA, free schools in Sweden and academies in England – this book provides a set of recommendations that offer a timely warning against the fragmentation of school systems in the misguided belief that competition benefits all children. It suggests that a more sensible approach would be to avoid situations whereby the improvement of one school leads to a decline in the resources available to, and subsequently the performance of, others.

At an important moment in global, political and educational change, the accounts presented in this book will be valuable not only to teachers, but also to those researching or working with education policy, politics and systems. It will be of interest therefore to those in governments, local authorities and other organisations involved in the improvement of schools and education systems, but who seek to do so in ways that reduce the inequities in our schools, as well as increase their performance.

Mel Ainscow is Professor of Education and Co-Director of the Centre for Equity in Education in the School of Education at the University of Manchester, UK.

Alan Dyson is Professor of Education and Co-Director of the Centre for Equity in Education in the School of Education at the University of Manchester, UK.

Sue Goldrick is a Researcher for the Centre for Equity in Education in the School of Education at the University of Manchester, UK.

Mel West is Professor of Educational Leadership and Head of the School of Education at the University of Manchester, UK.

Developing Equitable Education Systems

Mel Ainscow, Alan Dyson,
Sue Goldrick and Mel West

Routledge
Taylor & Francis Group

LONDON AND NEW YORK

First published 2012
by Routledge
2 Park Square, Milton Park, Abingdon, Oxon OX14 4RN

Simultaneously published in the USA and Canada
by Routledge
711 Third Avenue, New York, NY 10017

Routledge is an imprint of the Taylor & Francis Group, an informa business

British Library Cataloguing in Publication Data
A catalogue record for this book is available from the British Library

Library of Congress Cataloging in Publication Data
Developing equitable education systems / Mel Ainscow ... [et al.].
   p. cm.
   Includes bibliographical references and index.
   1. Educational equalization–Great Britain. 2. Children with social disabilities–
   Education–Great Britain. 3. Education and state–Great Britain.
   4. Educational change–Great Britain. I. Ainscow, Mel.
   LC213.3.G7D48 2012
   379.2'60941–dc23
   2011028885

ISBN: 978–0–415–61460–3 (hbk)
ISBN: 978–0–415–61461–0 (pbk)
ISBN: 978–0–203–81807–7 (ebk)

Typeset in Garamond
by Swales & Willis Ltd, Exeter, Devon

MIX
Paper from
responsible sources
FSC® C004839
www.fsc.org

Printed and bound in Great Britain by the MPG Books Group

Contents

Preface   vii

1 The challenge of equity in education   1

2 Using evidence to promote more equitable practice in schools   17

3 The development of an equity research network   37

4 Making schools more equitable   61

5 Making sense of the process   85

6 Assessing the impact   111

7 Drawing out the lessons   127

8 Rethinking the tasks   149

   References   167
   Index   175

Preface

As we worked on this book we were occasionally reminded of Kurt Lewin's often-quoted adage, *the best way to understand an organisation is by trying to change it.* The organisation that we were focused on was the English education system and the unequal ways in which it responds to children and young people. The focus of our efforts to bring about change was informed by the principle of equity, which we take to be broadly about inclusion and fairness.

The project we describe involved a network within which school practitioners and university researchers – and sometimes students – worked in partnership. What we learnt from these efforts left us to be generally optimistic and occasionally pessimistic.

Our sense of optimism was generated by the enthusiasm and commitment of the staff of the schools. What struck us most was the level of their professionalism and their willingness to go the extra mile for their students. In this respect, we saw compelling evidence of how groups of teachers – and support staff – could carry out inquiries that stimulated innovations into ways of engaging hard-to-reach groups of learners. We also saw how partnerships within and between schools helped to create the climate within which such innovations could take place.

Our occasional bouts of pessimism arose from the frustrations of the practitioners as they found their efforts restricted by contextual factors that were largely outside their control. In particular, we became increasingly aware of how national policies limited the space for developing new ways of working. More specifically, we saw the negative impact of the intense competition that is created between schools as a result of the emphasis placed on school autonomy and parental choice.

Whilst the project we describe was set within the English education system, we believe that the argument we develop is of wider relevance, not least because it emphasises the importance of contextual analysis as a means of determining locally defined strategies. Within the particular context that we describe, this drew attention to the factors that cause inequities to occur and pinpointed resources that could be mobilised in order to overcome these factors. It also helped us understand the need to rethink the tasks involved in a way that has implications for stakeholders at all levels of a school system.

Given the collaborative nature of the work we describe, it is inevitable that many colleagues have contributed to the ideas we present. Whilst it is impossible to thank each one individually, we must acknowledge the important contributions of the head teachers, staffs and students of the fourteen partner schools. Thanks must also be given to various colleagues at the University of Manchester who contributed in various ways to the project, particularly Joanna Bragg, Chris Chapman, David da Costa, David Hauk, Andy Howes, Denise Kasperkiewicz, Kirstin Kerr, Susie Miles, Diana Pearson and Carlo Raffo. We are also grateful for the work carried out in the schools by some of our graduate students, particularly Annita Eliadou, Dimitrina Kaneva and Danielle White. Finally, we must recognise the involvement of the Centre for Equity in Education's thinktank, the members of which took part in regular debates about the meaning and significance of our experiences within the network.

Mel Ainscow, Alan Dyson, Sue Goldrick and Mel West
University of Manchester
June 2011

1 The challenge of equity in education

This book is about equity in education. More particularly, it is about the efforts of a group of schools in England to develop more equitable practices and pro vision through a process of structured inquiry. These schools faced multiple challenges to this project arising from the sharp socio-economic and ethnic divisions in the populations they served, and a set of national education poli cies within which concerns about equity often seemed to be low down the list of priorities.

Educationalists in many countries will recognise the situation faced by these schools – requirements to drive standards of students' attainment ever higher; pressure to compete against other schools to secure more students and acquire additional funding; tight accountability for the achievement of narrow targets, with dire consequences for failure; deep divisions between those student who could flourish in schools and those who could not; and the apparent impossibility of equalising outcomes between these two groups. In this context, the commitment of these schools to educational equity was a brave step. They could easily have contented themselves with focusing on improving test and examination scores, as many other schools did. Not surprisingly too, the schools struggled with their task. In inquiring into their current practices, they uncovered problems and issues that some members of their staffs would no doubt have preferred to leave uncovered, whilst changing their practices proved fraught with difficulty.

Nonetheless, some of them at least looked unflinchingly at the issues that faced them and persevered to make their provision better for students who had previously found themselves marginalised in a range of ways. The outcomes were certainly not dramatic, but they do provide reason for optimism. They show that, even in unpromising situations, teachers and their colleagues in schools can learn new things about themselves, and can change in ways that benefit their most vulnerable students. It may indeed be the case that equitable developments in education will ultimately depend on governments being prepared to commit themselves to developing powerful pro-equity policy frameworks. In the meantime, it is also the case that much can be achieved by school change, and it should never be forgotten that even the most powerful policy frameworks require the intelligent commitment of teachers and schools.

What is equity?

Equity is a term that many people involved in education feel comfortable using but which few would be prepared to define in detail. If we want to talk about equity more colloquially, we might simply refer to 'fairness' – but this hardly helps us define what is and is not fair. We know that equity is somehow linked to social justice, to human (particularly, children's) rights, and to notions of equality. Some might think that equity is also linked to notions of inclusion, or gender equality, or multiculturalism. However, it is one thing to say that these ideas are linked, but quite another to say *how*, precisely, they are linked.

The position we take in this book is that a sense of fairness, however ill-defined, is a powerful starting point for schools to enquire into their own practice and provision. Many scholarly texts have been written which try to articulate one or other theory of equity. These texts have their place, but they are unlikely to provide useful starting points for most practitioners as they go about developing their work. Even if teachers were inclined to engage with these formulations (and some, no doubt, do), they can easily seem abstract and unrelated to the complex issues that they face in their classrooms. Our view is that it is much more productive for teachers to begin with a broad sense of what is fair and unfair, and to refine their understandings in context, by looking at what happens in their own schools and classrooms.

It makes sense, therefore, to start with some examples of the kinds of issues that teachers and their colleagues in schools frequently encounter. These examples are based on real situations taken from schools in England. If they were taken from other countries – from the USA, say, or from South Africa, or from China – the details would certainly be different since the education systems in those countries and the characteristics of their societies would generate different issues. Cultural notions of what is and is not 'fair' would offer teachers different lenses through which to see those issues. However, there are, we suggest, enough similarities for teachers in these different contexts at least to start a dialogue with each other about what they mean by equity.

The case of Henrik

Henrik is an 8-year-old boy who has made a successful and happy start to his school career in his home town in central Europe. However, the country he comes from is relatively poor and there are few well-paid work opportunities. His father, therefore, decided to move the family to England so that he can find work, at least in the medium term. They have moved to a town where there is a shortage of workers with his skills and have found some cheap accommodation close to a number of other families that have moved from their home country.

Having been enrolled in the local primary school, Henrik can make little sense of the lessons since he speaks almost no English. The school does not have a member of staff who can speak Henrik's language. The best that it can offer is to sit him next to a classmate who comes from the same country and speaks a little more English than he does. Together, they try to find their way through the lessons, but Henrik's educational progress has come to a halt, and he is now very unhappy at school.

The case of Julie

Julie is a 13-year-old girl who has grown up on a poor social housing estate on the outskirts of a major city. Her family is somewhat chaotic. Her father left long ago and her mother has had a succession of boyfriends, some of whom have treated her and the other children very badly. Julie's older brothers are constantly in trouble with the police and drug misuse is common in the home. Her educational attainments are low, but despite this, she enjoyed her time at primary school. Although she could in principle have chosen any one of a number of secondary schools in the area, the reality was very different. As far as she and her mother were concerned, the other schools were ruled out because they were for 'posh kids', or were full of children from ethnic minorities, or were faith schools. It never really occurred to either of them that Julie should go anywhere other than to the school on the estate – the same school that her mother had attended.

Julie's time at her new school was not without its problems. She missed a lot of schooling, and ended up in fights with other students, or in quarrels with her teachers. Despite this, the school did all it could to support her, and she came to see it as something of a refuge from her turbulent home life. However, the school itself was in difficulties because of its consistently poor academic results, the problems it had in retaining high-quality staff, and its declining roll as other, more apparently successful schools competed for students. Eventually, the local authority decided to close the school down. Julie and her mother were offered a choice of other schools to attend and chose the one some of Julie's friends also chose, a few miles away. Unfortunately, she received little of the support in her new school that she had previously enjoyed, and she found herself being bullied by some of its existing students. That, together with the long bus journey to get to school, impacted on her attendance, which became very erratic. In effect, she has ceased to learn anything in school, and does not feel comfortable in the home, so she spends much of her time walking round the estate with a group of other girls whose attendance is equally poor.

The case of Linda

Like Julie, Linda is 13 years old. Like Julie also, her family have relatively little money. However, the family is stable, home is a safe place, and Linda has always been encouraged by her parents to try her best at school. In fact, she has come to realise over the years that her attainments are nothing very special. She has no obvious difficulties, but neither does she shine at anything. She is probably not helped by the fact that she is a shy girl who does not like to draw attention to herself. At primary school she liked her class teacher, who made a point of spending time with her and who went out of her way to tell her parents how she was doing.

At secondary school things are different. The school operates a policy of grouping students by levels of attainment and, for most subjects, Linda is in one of the lower sets. Some of her friends get taken out of lessons for extra help, but Linda does not. Instead, she goes from lesson to lesson and keeps her head down. Some of the boys in her classes take up most of the teachers' attention, and there is little opportunity for Linda to get to know them, or for them to get to know Linda. She is content enough at school, but she is making little progress. Her parents know little about what her school life is really like, and are happy that she appears to be keeping out of trouble and has no obvious problems.

Reflecting on the cases

Anyone who has worked in and around schools would be able to think of children like these. In each case, there is something that is likely to strike most people as unfair. Sometimes, the unfairness is gross. It cannot be right, for example, that Henrik is expected to learn in a language he cannot understand. It is obviously unfair that Julie's schooling is disrupted by decisions over which she has no control. Sometimes – as in Linda's case – the unfairness is more subtle. She has no overwhelming problems at school, but there is nonetheless something unfair in the lack of attention she receives, and in the disproportionate attention that goes to the boys in her class. When we set what is happening to these children against an ideal of school as a place where all children learn and develop – and a place where every child has an equal chance to do so – the unfairness is obvious.

To some extent, the unfair treatment of these children could be overcome if their teachers and school were more aware of what was happening to them, and more able to take steps to put things right. It would not take much for Linda's teachers to speak to her a little more, or for her school to set up some sort of guidance system to ensure that all children had a friendly adult to whom they could relate. It might not take much more for Henrik's school to find an adult who could speak his language, or a teacher who could help him develop his English. However, not every problem can be attributed to the schools. It costs money for schools to employ specialist language or guidance staff – money that might be needed, say, to employ more subject teachers or teaching assistants so that the school can achieve performance targets set for it by central government. In any case, Julie's original secondary school seems to have made a very good job of helping her with her multiple problems. It is not the school's fault any more than it is Julie's that decision-makers in central and local government have opted to close the school down, or that competitor schools helped to hasten its spiral of decline.

Some of the problems experienced by these young people can be located beyond the education system. Linda's parents have themselves not had the educational experience to understand how schools work, or what is really needed for young people to do well in the education system. As with many working class families, their ambitions for their children are high, but their knowledge of how to achieve those ambitions is lower. In the same way, it is not the fault of the education system that Julie lives in such chaotic circumstances – though chaotic families are often (though not always) poor families, and poor families may well find themselves living alongside other poor families and sending their children to schools that are vulnerable to failure and closure. As for Henrik, his educational problems can be traced, ultimately, to the forces of economic globalisation that make some countries richer and other ones poorer, and which create flows of migrants from the latter to the former. However inadequate the response of his school, it is not the school's fault that Henrik is where he is.

Some frameworks for understanding equity

There are many other cases that could sit alongside the three presented here – children who do badly in education because they have an inadequate teacher, perhaps, or because they are bullied, or because they cannot get provision to meet their difficulties, or because they feel unwanted and unvalued, or because their ethnic or class group seems somehow to be at a disadvantage. All of these are inequities because they do not match the idea of an education system in which all children learn and develop. All of them are also likely to be complex in their causation. It may seem simple to attribute the problem to an 'inadequate teacher', but inadequate teachers can only survive where schools and education systems allow them to, and where families are not able to do something to help their children.

There is, then, a further layer of complexity when we ask ourselves how we would like to see these unfair situations changed. Do we want Henrik to be taught English, or to be taught in his native language – or do we think it should never have been necessary for his family to move to another country in order to find work? Do we want Linda to be spoken to more often, or do we want to do something to make her achievements like those of her more successful peers, and to equip her parents – and others like them – to support their children's schooling more effectively? As for Julie, do we want her school to stay open, or her new school to offer better support? Or do we want some kind of fundamental social reform that would somehow overcome the problems of poor estates and chaotic families?

The view we take in this book is that it is essential that such questions are asked – not least by educators – but that the answers to them are usually complex and contested. In working through these complexities, it is helpful to have some frameworks to guide our thinking. Frameworks of the kind we have in mind cannot provide easy answers to complex questions – but they can help sharpen the way in which questions are asked, and at least help start the process of thinking how they might be answered.

The overall framework we develop in this book looks at the way in which evident inequities can be traced back to their root causes. This leads us to argue that – as far as education is concerned – it is necessary to think of inequities with respect to *within-school, between-schools*, and *beyond-school factors*. More specifically:

> **Within-school** inequities can be attributed to the practices and structures of schools themselves – to how teachers operate, how the school groups students, how it responds to diversity and so on. Henrik's linguistic reliance on a classmate is, in the first instance at least, an in-school inequity.

> **Between-school** inequities arise in the school and wider education system. They relate to the way that school provision is organised in an area, the way that children find their way into different schools, and the opportunities that are or are not available in the area. The closing of Julie's school is, in the first instance, a system issue – that is, a between-schools inequity.

> Finally, **beyond-school** inequities arise from the socio-economic context within which schooling takes place. They are to do with social inequalities, poverty, global economics and the existence of neighbourhoods, towns and regions that are 'made poor'. All three of our cases experience inequities of this kind, and it is arguable that many, if not all of the inequities in education are ultimately traceable to these underlying factors.

Other frameworks are useful when we begin to ask not where inequities arise, but what we mean by equity and inequity. The philosopher of social justice, Nancy Fraser, usefully points to three interacting dimensions of what we are here calling equity – *distribution, recognition and representation* (Fraser, 2008). The first of these is probably the one that is most familiar in thinking about educational equity. In most (probably, all) education systems, educational resources, opportunities and outcomes are *distributed* in ways that many observers would regard as unfair. In our case studies, for instance, Julie is a classic example of a child whose educational opportunities and outcomes are shaped not by any individual merits she may or may not have, but by factors in her social background over which she has no control. We might say the same of Linda and Henrik, but we can also see here the issue of how far the cultural identities of these children are *recognised* by their schools and the school system. In Henrik's case, there is a stark failure even to recognise his language as a medium of instruction. However, it is equally true that Linda's 'way of being' in school is one that the school is unable to acknowledge and build upon. In terms of *representation*, moreover, it goes without saying that none of the three children – and, indeed, none of their parents – has any effective say in what happens to them. The school system places them and treats them more or less as it wishes, and even if there are, in principle, opportunities for them to take control (by choosing other schools, for instance), the reality is that their ability to exercise those choices is extremely limited.

Fraser's framework is particularly useful because it broadens the focus of equity concerns beyond questions of distribution. In the same way, Amartya Sen's notion of 'capability' encourages us to think about equity as being about more than who gets what (Sen, 1980, 2009). Again put very simply, Sen argues that the distribution of resources has to be considered alongside the question of what it is that resources enable people to do – their *capabilities*. People take a view, whether explicitly or otherwise, about what they value in terms of what they do and how they are able to live. What matters is their capability – to achieve the kinds of lives they value. Material and other resources may certainly help, but simply distributing resources more fairly does not ensure that everyone can achieve the kinds of lives they want. Looked at in this way, it seems likely that the indifferent educational experiences available to Julie, Henrik and Linda will limit the real choices they have about how they wish to live. More particularly, the education system in which they are required to participate is not one that is based around any exploration of what they value, or any systematic attempt to build their capabilities for achieving what they want. Instead, it is built on a series of normal expectations about what counts as educational success and how educational success will lead on to a 'successful' life. The issue, therefore, may not be simply that these three children do less well than some of their peers, but that even those apparently successful peers are constrained by the definitions of success built into the system.

Needless to say, the notions of capability, redistribution, recognition and representation are far more complex than we have presented them here. They could, moreover, be further elaborated by many other equity-related concepts – for instance, notions of equality, or rights, or democracy, or inclusion. However, even this cursory analysis suggests some powerful ways in which equity issues can be explored. Asking the broad question 'is this equitable?' also means asking:

- *Who gets what?* How are educational opportunities, resources and outcomes distributed between individuals and across groups? Are there justifiable reasons for that distribution, or is it arbitrary, or shaped by factors that should play no part?
- *Who is treated in what way?* Beyond the distribution of resources, how far are learners valued equally? Are their differences respected and welcomed, or is there a hierarchy of valuing in which some characteristics and cultures are more welcome than others?
- *Who can do what?* Who has the power to make decisions, and how far can learners shape what happens to them? Beyond this, does the education system enable learners to be and do what they value, or does it place limits on the real choices that some – perhaps many – can choose to make?

These are certainly not the only questions that can be asked about equity, but they are, as we shall see throughout this book, a powerful starting point.

Educational equity in England

Every country has its own forms of equity and inequity. There are many countries which, on the face of it, do worse in this respect than England, but also many that do better. Moreover, the salient issues in each country are likely to be somewhat different, and depend on the cultural, historical and political forces that shape different societies. The United States, for instance, is shaped, amongst many other things, by its history of slavery, segregation and civil rights. Other countries are shaped by histories of colonisation and by the global processes of the post-colonial order. England, by contrast, has been shaped – again, amongst many other things – by a history of imperialism, by its leading position in the industrial revolution, and by the processes of economic and social change as imperialism and industry have waned.

From inside the country, it is sometimes easy to forget the many ways in which England can claim to be equitable – particularly in respect of its educational provision. England is an affluent, democratic country. It has ample resources to sustain a high-quality education system, and democratic control of that system – however imperfect – ensures that some attention is paid to the equitable distribution of those resources. Indeed, the country has a tradition of welfarism stretching back beyond the landmark Beveridge report during the Second World War which means that the state accepts responsibility for the well-being of its citizens, and for ameliorating the disadvantages that some of those citizens may experience (Beveridge, 1942). In education terms, this means that there has been universal elementary education for a century and a half, extended progressively to the secondary phase, and with increasing participation in tertiary education. As educational participation has increased, there have also been repeated efforts to extend educational integration. The large majority of children, for instance, attend state rather than private schools, the majority of these are non-selective (at least by 'ability'), and the separation of learners into different tracks is avoided through all of primary and much of secondary education. There is also a well-resourced special education sector that enables additional support resources to be available in ordinary schools and classrooms, and for many decades there have been significant efforts to support the lowest performing learners and institutions.

Despite these positives, there remain deep-seated inequalities in English society as a whole, and in its education system in particular (Wilkinson and Pickett, 2000). A recent review set out in troubling detail the inequalities which beset the country and, specifically, the ways these inequalities are associated with gender, ethnicity, disability and socio-economic status (Equality and Human Rights Commission, 2010). These inequalities are certainly evident in the English education system,[1] and have persisted despite the (sometimes strenuous) efforts of successive governments to address them. A running sore in the system, for instance, is that educational outcomes are powerfully shaped by learners' socio-economic background (Schools Analysis and Research Division, 2009). Put simply, the poorer the family, the less chance children have of achieving well at school and enjoying a sustained and successful educational career. Moreover, although differences in attainments are evident well before children enter school, there is no evidence that the school system succeeds in closing this gap.

Although socio-economic status is the major determinant of outcomes, it interacts with other factors, notably gender and ethnicity. However, the patterns are far from simple. Although in broad terms it is true that girls outperform

1 The Commission's report refers to the United Kingdom as a whole, of which England is by far the most populous part. However, each of the four administrations in the UK – England, Northern Ireland, Scotland and Wales – is responsible for its own education system. Although these systems are similar in many respects, there are important differences, and this book is located firmly in the English context.

boys and white students outperform many other ethnic groups (Gillborn and Mirza, 2000), this disguises a complex set of interactions. In particular, it hides the relatively high performance of some non-white groups and the relatively low performance of some parts of the white population (DfES, 2005; Goodman *et al.*, 2009). Moreover, there are many other factors at work to explain differences in attainment. Particularly relevant to the focus of this book is the spatial dimension in unequal outcomes. Put simply, place matters in education (Lupton, 2006). There are concentrations of children from particular backgrounds (notably, socio-economic status and ethnicity) in particular places in the UK and accordingly outcomes vary by place. Again, in crude terms, many children from poor backgrounds are concentrated in areas characterised by a range of social problems. The schools serving those areas therefore face significant challenges, and some of them struggle or find themselves unable to cope (Thrupp and Lupton, 2006). Poor children, therefore, already at risk of poor outcomes, may find themselves trapped in schools that are effectively unable to help them.

The focus on the relationship between social background and outcomes has tended to dominate thinking about educational equity in England for many years. However, the distribution of outcomes is only one form of educational inequity in this country. There are also issues around the distribution of opportunities. This goes beyond the challenges faced by schools serving areas of deprivation to include the persistence both of a private, fee-paying sector and of hierarchies of schools in different areas. It remains possible for affluent families to buy places in private schools that are generally well-resourced and high status, and which, of course, face none of the challenges in terms of disadvantage that confront state schools.

On a larger scale, schools that select by academic 'ability' (known traditionally as grammar schools) persist in certain places, whilst most areas have a hierarchy of higher and lower status schools. If learners from poor socio-economic backgrounds tend to be concentrated in low-status schools, higher-status schools tend to take less than their 'fair' share of such students, regardless of whether they select overtly or not (The Sutton Trust, 2005). There is a particular issue around so-called 'faith' schools. The state education system in England has large numbers of schools that are run by faith groups – notably the Church of England and the Roman Catholic Church. Although these schools must follow the guidance and regulations applying to all other state schools, they are allowed to select students by the religious faith of their families. This in itself is sometimes seen as socially divisive. However, there is also evidence that in some cases selection by faith is used as a cover for selection by other socially desirable characteristics (West *et al.*, 2009).

There is a further set of issues around the special education system. Despite decades of efforts to promote first 'integration' and then 'inclusion', England retains a segregated sector of special schools, educating about one per cent of the school population. Added to this is a much larger (but unquantifiable) sector of semi-segregated provision in the form of special classes, resource bases and alternative forms of provision in and around regular schools. Although the debates around inclusive education are sometimes fierce in England, the reality is that a significant minority of learners in the English system do not have access to the same forms of provision as the majority of their peers. This is, of course, an issue in the distribution of educational opportunities and outcomes. However, many inclusion advocates would argue that it is also an issue in recognition and representation (see, for instance, Booth and Ainscow, 2002).

To this extent, there are similar recognition and representation issues around how the English education system responds to the ethnic diversity of the population. Despite many decades of experience in including diverse ethnic groups within the education system, whilst respecting the diversity of those groups, so-called 'multiculturalism' remains a controversial endeavour, even amongst senior politicians (Cameron, 2011). Moreover, the concentrations of particular ethnic groups in particular places sometimes result in a de facto segregation in schools (Johnston *et al.*, 2006). The poisonous cocktail of residential segregation leading to and reinforced by school segregation has, from time to time, had explosive consequences (Cantle, 2001). More generally, however, the de facto segregation of schools by ethnicity denies access to shared opportunities and resources, and makes any notion of equal valuing highly problematic.

Equity and education policy in England

The list of educational inequities in England could be expanded well beyond the ones offered above. However, it is important to recognise that policy-makers have been by no means unaware of these issues and have repeatedly tried to tackle them. There have been particular efforts over the past decade and a half, where a succession of education ministers in centre-left New Labour governments have committed themselves to tackling various aspects of educational inequity (see, for instance, Blunkett, 1999; Kelly, 2005). Whether these efforts have been adequate is a matter for debate. Suffice it to say, whilst they have almost certainly made the situation much better than it might otherwise have been, they have been insufficient to enable the English education system to claim that it is built solely on principles of equity.

It is our contention that the word 'solely' is particularly important in understanding the successes and failures of efforts to tackle inequity. The New Labour governments from 1997-2010 (that is the governments in power when the work reported elsewhere in this book was in progress) certainly tried to tackle at least some aspects of educational inequity. However, that is by no means all they tried to do. The contradictions between different agendas go some way to explain the limitations of equity-oriented policies. At the same time, it also explains why spaces opened up at the local level in which teachers and their schools could develop their own responses to the issues with which they were confronted.

New Labour governments were notoriously hyperactive in terms of the policy initiatives they launched, and it is impossible to give a full account of these here (see various chapters in Chapman and Gunter, 2009, for a fuller explanation). However, it is arguable that there were two main policy thrusts in education, summed up neatly in the stated aim of achieving 'excellence for the many, not just for the few' (Blunkett, 1999). One thrust was around the drive for excellence, understood as constantly improving levels of performance across the school system as a whole. When elected in 1997, New Labour inherited from the outgoing Conservative government a system that was marked by a combination of central control and marketisation. Schools had to teach what they were told by central government, were held to account for the attainments of their students, and were rigorously scrutinised by Ofsted (The Office for Standards in Education), the national schools inspectorate. At the same time, they were encouraged to compete against one another to recruit new students, not least because they managed their own budgets, and every additional student brought more funding.

Far from rethinking these approaches, in their pursuit of 'excellence' New Labour governments set about strengthening them. As a result, central prescription increased: at one stage teachers were instructed not only on the broad content of curriculum, but on the design and minute-by-minute content of lessons; penalties for 'failure' became tougher; and the range of different 'types' of schools was expanded to increase the choice that families notionally had in deciding where to have their children educated. Of particular significance for part of our story in this book are the draconian measures that ensued should a school fail to perform at what were regarded as acceptable levels. Such schools could be closed and at various times (the policies changed frequently), opened as new schools, 'federated with' more apparently successful schools, or were replaced by 'academies'. The latter were a new form of independent state school, similar in many ways to charter schools in the United States and free schools in Sweden (Meyland-Smith and Evans, 2009). Outside the control of local authorities (local democratic bodies responsible for schools as well as a range of other public services), and with private individuals and groups acting as controlling 'sponsors', academies came to be seen as the central strategy for improving poorly performing schools (see the chapters in Gunter, 2011, for a range of perspectives on this controversial policy).

Whether these actions produced the 'world class' school system that ministers avowed they were aiming for is a matter of some debate (see, for instance,

The Primary Review, 2007). However, it is clear that they had some perverse consequences in relation to the equity of the system. Perhaps the best way to sum up these consequences is through the notion of 'performativity' that has sometimes been used to describe the overall thrust of policy (Ball, 2003; Broadfoot, 2001). In essence, the complex business of education, with its multiple aims and its attention to diverse learners, was reduced to a matter of performing to required levels on a narrow range of performance measures. Put crudely, what children learnt and how they developed was less important than whether they could pass tests; how different groups and individuals did was less important than whether enough students moved from just below arbitrary benchmark levels (referred to as 'floor targets' or, more recently, as 'floor standards') to just above them for the school to escape punishment; and whether all children in an area had good provision and good outcomes was less important to schools than whether they individually were successful, even if that meant beggaring their neighbours. The incentives on schools – which, to be fair, many resisted – were not to do well by all children, but to recruit high-performing students, and focus their efforts on those around benchmark levels, whilst studiously avoiding low-attaining, troublesome, or 'needy' children.

Despite this gloomy portrait, it in fact only tells half of the New Labour story. From the start, the government's domestic policy was informed by a desire to tackle 'social exclusion' (Social Exclusion Unit, 2001). If there was to be an improvement in overall social and educational conditions, this should be accompanied by efforts to ensure that vulnerable groups and individuals were not excluded from the benefits of these improvements. In educational terms, this translated into a series of initiatives aimed at 'narrowing the gap' between the poorest-performing students and the rest (DCSF IDeA and LGA, 2007). These were wide-ranging, diverse and (some might argue) incoherent, but they included efforts targeted at poorly-performing individuals, groups and institutions. For the most part, they were conceived narrowly as being about raising levels of measured attainments, or improving the performance of students and their schools on some other performance measure. To this extent, equity-oriented interventions simply formed part of a continuum of interventions within the overall push for 'excellence'. For instance, New Labour introduced national literacy and numeracy strategies aimed at raising overall standards of attainment in these areas in primary schools but with a series of increasingly powerful interventions for students who fell behind their peers (DfES, 2001b).

However, by no means was everything New Labour did quite so straightforwardly instrumental. To take an example, New Labour governments took legislative action to strengthen the position of children with special educational needs and disabilities in regular schools (DfES, 2001a). It became more difficult for schools to discriminate wilfully against such children, and correspondingly easier for them to be 'included' in the mainstream. This may well have had something to do with ensuring that such children could participate in the excellence agenda, but it also owed much to concerns about the place of disabled children in society – in other words, about their 'recognition'.

A second, even more wide-ranging development was the introduction of what became known as the *Every Child Matters* agenda (DfES, 2003). Through a series of legislative changes and policy initiatives, the government sought to align a range of child and family services around a coherent attempt to promote child well-being. From the point of view of schools, this meant that they were expected to work closely with other agencies, offer a range of additional (and often non-educational) services and activities to their students, and involve themselves with families and communities. Above all, they were expected to widen their focus from narrow questions of educational attainment to encompass children's health, well-being, safety, life chances and place in society. As the implications of this agenda emerged, it turned into an overarching vision of a 'Twenty-First Century school' (DCSF, 2008), one that was to play a far-reaching role in the lives of children, families and communities. Again, it is not difficult to see how this approach might contribute to the excellence agenda by other means. At the same time, however, it implied a much more wide-ranging view of what kinds of inequities might appear in children's lives, and from where in those lives they might arise.

The school perspective

At the start of this chapter, we explored issues of educational equity and inequity through the experiences of three fictional – but not entirely untypical – children. However, the focus of this book is not on children directly, but on the schools they attend and the teachers who work in those schools. This is not accidental. The touchstone of the extent to which an education system is equitable is what happens to the learners within it. The experiences of children are, therefore, central to the concerns of this book, and, as we shall see, efforts to understand those experiences were central to how many of the schools in the project we describe – the Stockborough Equity Research Network – pursued their inquiries and developments. However, schools and teachers are crucial too, for it is they who are in a position to make the most immediate difference to learners' experiences. What, then, was the situation facing schools and teachers in England as this project began?

By 2006, schools had already experienced a decade and a half of extensive educational reform. Those reforms had sought (often successfully) to focus the efforts of teachers on a narrow set of performance targets at the expense of wider educational concerns, or concerns about the diverse population of

learners. The degree of central prescription was massive, the level of surveillance of teachers' work was high, and the penalties for 'failure' were potentially
severe. At the same time, as we have explained, schools were operating in a
socially and educationally unequal context. Those serving relatively advantaged
populations could feel reasonably secure. However, many schools serving more
disadvantaged populations faced a constant struggle to drive overall levels of
attainment up to accepted levels, to deal with the range of social problems
washing into the school from its area environment, to attract new students, and
generally to avoid falling foul of punitive accountability regimes. If they sometimes acted in the interests of institutional survival rather than the well-being of
their students, this is hardly surprising.

At the same time, all schools were being invited – and in some respects
required – to consider issues of social and educational equity. They were subject to some legal requirements and a great deal of exhortation to pay attention
to those students most at risk of marginalisation. If they were serving disadvantaged populations, the chances are they would be bombarded by initiatives
(usually carrying both additional requirements and additional resources) aimed
at tackling this or that equity issue. Often, too, those initiatives would expect
schools to turn their gaze outwards, to forego their preoccupation with their
own performance, and to take part in collective action with other schools and
other agencies.

Above all, given the rapid succession of initiatives, and the tensions – if not
outright contradictions – within policy, schools had to make sense of a complex and rapidly changing landscape. Despite the high levels of central prescription, they still had to find their own way to salvation. They had to decide how
best to raise their overall game, how to reconcile this with the need to intervene
with marginalised groups, and how far to engage with wider issues in the lives
of their students, and of their families and communities. Perhaps more than
ever, school leaders – and, particularly, head teachers – came to play a dominant
role in charting the direction to be taken. It was they who had to manage the
school as a more-or-less autonomous institution, balancing its budget, hiring
and leading its staff, and carrying the can when things went wrong. It was they
who had to ensure that government directives were implemented and government targets met. More particularly, it was they who had to decide how the
complexities and contradictions of policy would be worked out in practice, and
to do so in a way that would avoid destabilising their school.

Conclusion

What follows in the remainder of this book is in one sense an account of a
small-scale development project involving a number of schools in an attempt

to explore and address equity issues. No doubt for most of these schools it was just one more of the many things they chose or were required to do. In another sense, however, the project is a searchlight shone into the innermost workings of the schools, as their teachers, support staff and heads sought to navigate the stormy seas in which they found themselves.

In the next chapter, we summarise the ideas that informed our thinking as we set out to design the project. In the main, these ideas emerged from our involvement in earlier initiatives that had adopted an inquiry-based approach to school development, using notions of networking and collaboration that involved groups of schools supported by teams of academic researchers. Chapter 3 explains how these ideas were introduced into schools in 'Stockborough' and then refined through processes of collaborative development and research. The two chapters that follow – 4 and 5 – use accounts of what happened in these schools to illustrate the approach in action, and to throw light on its potential and some of the difficulties involved.

Chapter 6 analyses the impact of these processes on the schools, their students and staff. This leads us to reflect on what can be learnt from these experiences, specifically about the empowering of staff-led inquiry groups as a school improvement strategy and, more generally, about achieving more equitable educational provision. Continuing with this process of analysis, Chapter 7 focuses on the limitations of the approach developed in Stockborough. This leads us to argue that the complex processes at work in the schools are linked within what we define as an *ecology of equity*. This suggests that the extent to which students' experiences and outcomes are equitable is not dependent only on the educational practices of their teachers, or even their schools. Instead, it depends on a whole range of interacting processes that reach into the school from outside. As a result, we propose a series of organisational conditions that are needed in order that education systems can move in a more equitable direction. Finally, in Chapter 8 we summarise the implications of our analysis in terms of the way the various stakeholders carry out their respective tasks.

2 Using evidence to promote more equitable practice in schools

Over the last twenty years or so, members of our team have been involved in a series of projects that have sought to address the challenges discussed in the previous chapter. Through this extensive experience, an approach that involves using forms of inquiry to address issues of equity within education systems has gradually emerged.

In this chapter, we describe and analyse these earlier experiences of working with networks of schools, in order to explain how this shaped the thinking that informed the project that is the main focus of our attention in this book. Specifically, we discuss two earlier initiatives, *'Improving the Quality of Education for All'* and *'Understanding and Developing Inclusive Practices in Schools'*. Before doing this, however, we say a little more about efforts to use research to promote educational equity within the national context in which our work has developed, and how this context has shaped our approach.

Researching equity

Like many other countries, England has been making extensive efforts to improve the quality of its public education system. Over the last few years this has involved a series of national reforms (see chapters in Chapman and Gunter, 2009, for a summary and critique of these developments). As we have monitored the impact of these initiatives, we have remained concerned about their effects on certain groups of learners, particularly those from economically disadvantaged backgrounds (Ainscow *et al.*, 2006). In particular, we have documented how the development of an educational market place, coupled with an emphasis on policies fostering greater diversity between schools, has created a quasi-selective system in which the poorest children, by and large, attend the lowest-performing schools.

This has led us to argue that these policies have increased rather than decreased disparities in education quality and opportunity between advantaged and less privileged groups. Giroux and Schmidt (2004) explain how similar reform policies in the United States have turned some schools into 'test-prep centres'. As a result, such schools tend to be increasingly ruthless in their disregard of those students who pose a threat to their 'success', as determined by standardised assessment procedures.

Educational research has had much to say about the disjuncture between reform efforts and equitable outcomes (Ball, 2008; Kerr and West, 2010). However, there is a strong sense amongst researchers that, too often, their contributions are ignored by policy-makers whenever they become too critical. More generally, there has been much concern in England that policy and practice communities on the one hand, and the research community on the other, have no robust structures through which they can communicate, and in any case, do not speak the same language even when they do make contact. Put simply, researchers fail to produce findings upon which actions can be based, while policy-makers and practitioners fail to inform their actions with such research evidence as is available (Hillage *et al.*, 1998).

In this situation, there have been numerous efforts to bring research, policy and practice closer together. At a structural level, for instance, some years ago there was an attempt by the government in England to establish a National Education Research Forum that would bring researchers, policy-makers and practitioners together to identify key issues, create mechanisms for communication, and, ultimately to generate applied research that practitioners could understand and use. The forum became interested in how the form and orientation of research activity might make it more or less user-friendly. In particular, it focused on *research and development* as a term to describe an ongoing interaction between research and the formation of policy and practice (NERF, 2000, 2001). In so doing, it was tapping into a tradition across a wide range of applied research disciplines, in which research would set out to investigate problems generated by practice, practitioners would implement the findings of research, and that implementation process would itself be researched so that solutions might be refined. This was intended to lead to a cyclical process in which research, implementation and adaptation would follow closely upon one another, and the barriers between research and practice would be eroded (Cobb *et al.*, 2003; Hargreaves, 1999). There have been similar conceptualisations in the USA, not least those in so-called 'design-based research' (The Design-Based Research Collective, 2003).

Closely related to research and development is the well-established tradition of *educational action research* (Carr and Kemmis, 1986; Ebbutt, 1985; Elliott, 1991; Kemmis and McTaggart, 1988; Oja and Smulyan, 1989). In England, as in many other countries, action research has enjoyed periods of considerable prominence as a means of bringing research and practice together, not least because of its adaptability as a broad approach, rather than as a precisely defined methodology. For instance, action research offers a means of understanding complex organisations by attempting to change them (Lewin, 1946), of stimulating change in organisations (Checkland, 1981; Checkland and Scholes, 1990), of understanding practitioner thinking (Eraut, 1994; McIntyre, 2005), or of enabling practitioners to better understand their practice from both a technical and a critical perspective (Armstrong and Moore, 2004; Carr and Kemmis, 1986; Elliott, 1991; O'Hanlon, 2003). Here the aim is to improve practice and understanding through a combination of systematic reflection and strategic innovation (Miles and Ainscow, 2011).

There are many similarities between approaches in the action research family and those in the research and development family. However, where they differ is in the relationship between research and action. Research and development approaches tend to find the solutions to the problems of practice outside the practice situation itself (for instance, in prior research or theorising) and then refine those solutions in the practice situation. Action research approaches, broadly speaking, begin by researching the practice situation to see what solutions might be found therein, and only later (if at all) systematise and theorise what they have found with a view to its transfer to other situations.

At a time when policy and practice are struggling with issues of equity, and where researchers feel they have something to contribute to these issues, attempts to bring research and practice together begin to seem particularly apposite. From the perspective of researchers, in particular, they open up the possibility that the distinctive forms of knowledge made available by robust research processes might at last be used to make the education system more efficient and effective, not just in a technical sense, but also more socially just. However, in reviewing established traditions of action research, and research and development, we found ourselves questioning just how far these two approaches can be used effectively to address challenges in education around issues of equity. There are a number of pressing concerns, not least around the following:

- The question of *engagement*. Although methods are available for bringing research, practice and policy closer together, there is no obvious reason why practitioners and policy-makers should engage with those methods.
- The question of *values*, and, related to that, the question of *power*. There is a strong tradition of critical research which stands outside policy and practice, and seeks to problematise the value systems and power relations that they embody. However, as research comes closer to policy and practice, it has to engage with the values and power relations embodied therein. Specifically, it has to find ways of engaging with and changing individuals and groups holding values different from those of the researcher and

quite possibly embedded in particular sets of power relations. Much action research and most research and development simply avoids this issue by treating change as a technical process.

- The question of *transfer*. Even where changes in policy and practice do result from engagement in research processes, how can such changes be made transferable? How useful are processes depending on intensive interactions between researchers, practitioners and policy-makers in particular situations, when inequity is endemic at the system level?

Our work is located at the heart of these concerns. We are committed to doing research that makes a difference in relation to educational equity. We seek, therefore, to impact on policy and practice where we can, and to adopt a social justice stance to justify these impacts. Moreover, we seek to have an impact on as large a scale as possible, which means moving from work with individual practitioners and institutions, to work with groups and systems, and, correspondingly, to move from work at the level of specific practices to work at the level of policy. In order to do so, it seems necessary to move from opportunistic engagements with practitioners and policy-makers towards the development of a robust set of processes – a methodology – which can be used consistently across a range of contexts and which, ideally, does not require the immediate presence of any particularly group of researchers.

In what follows, we discuss two earlier projects that helped to move our thinking and processes of engagement towards an approach that we now call *development and research*. As we move through these accounts, we will discuss the issues to which they give rise. This leads us to draw out a series of ideas that informed our involvement in the Stockborough project.

A school improvement project

Improving the Quality of Education for All (IQEA) began towards the end of the 1980s at the University of Cambridge as a small-scale school improvement project. Over many years it grew as a result of projects carried out within many school networks, both in the United Kingdom and overseas (see Ainscow, 1999; Clarke *et al.*, 2005; Hopkins, 2007; Hopkins *et al.*, 1994; Hopkins *et al.*, 1996; and West and Ainscow, 2010 for more detailed accounts of some of these projects). These networks involved teams of researchers working in partnership with colleagues from schools to identify ways in which the learning of all members of the school community – including students, parents and staff – could be enhanced. However, whilst the structures and practices of IQEA developed in the light of accumulating experience, its work continued to be guided by a consistent set of principles. These were as follows:

- The overriding focus for school improvement activity is to enhance the quality of student learning.
- The vision of the school should reflect this focus, and embrace all members of the school's community, both as learners and potential contributors.
- The school will find there are important opportunities to secure internal priorities in adapting to external pressures for change.
- The school will seek to develop structures and create conditions that encourage collaboration and lead to the empowerment of individuals and groups.
- The school will seek to promote the view that inquiry, and the monitoring and evaluation of quality, are responsibilities in which all members of staff share.

These principles, with their overall emphasis on collaboration amongst all members of a school community, provided touchstones for the development of improvement strategies. Schools that joined the various IQEA networks and projects were invited to use them to inform both their thinking and practices

The IQEA approach was based on an improvement model that emphasises the following features:

- The encouragement of developments in teaching and leadership practices, through the creation of conditions within schools for managing change successfully.
- The need for school improvement activities to be led from within school, focusing on areas that are seen to be matters of priority.
- The importance of collecting and engaging with evidence, in order to move thinking and practice forward, and to evaluate progress.
- The benefits of collaboration amongst colleagues from partner schools, and with IQEA researchers, so that a wider range of expertise and resources is available to support improvements in all of the participating schools.

Work with schools in the IQEA projects was based upon a *contract* that attempted to define the parameters for our involvement, and the obligations those involved owed to one another. In particular, the contract emphasised that all staff be consulted; that an in-school team of coordinators be appointed to carry the work forward; that a critical mass of staff were to be actively involved; and that sufficient time would be made available for necessary classroom and staff development activities. Meanwhile we committed ourselves to supporting the school's developments, usually in the first place for one year. Often the arrangement continued, however, and in some instances we were involved for periods as long as seven years. We provided training for the school coordinators, made regular school visits and contributed to school-based staff development activities. In addition, we attempted to work with the schools in recording and analysing their experiences in a way that also provided data relevant to our own ongoing research agendas. These data also contributed to our ongoing analysis of these developments.

The commitment to work with the schools in these ways presented us with a number of difficulties and dilemmas. In a more traditional project we might well have chosen to introduce to the school an established model of development based upon research carried out elsewhere. Then, having set the initiative going, our task would have been to stand back and record the process and outcomes of the intervention. In IQEA, we deliberately chose to adopt a very different approach, based upon an alternative perspective of how change can be understood and facilitated. Rather than seeking to impose externally validated models of improvement, we were seeking to support schools in creating their own models. Our assumption was that such an approach – that builds upon the biographies and circumstances of particular organisations – is much more likely to bring about and help sustain significant improvements in the quality of schooling. It follows, therefore, that we did not view school improvement as a 'quick-fix' business.

As a result of such engagements with schools involved in the IQEA project we evolved a style of collaboration that we referred to as 'working with, rather than working on'. This phrase attempted to sum up an approach that deliberately allows each project school considerable autonomy to determine its own priorities for development and, indeed, its methods for achieving these priorities. In attempting to work in this way, we found ourselves confronted with staggering complexity, and by a bewildering array of policy and strategy options. It was our belief, however, that only through a regular engagement with these complexities could a greater understanding of school improvement be achieved.

The overall framework used to guide activities within IQEA schools was conceptually simple (see Figure 2.1). Schools began by examining their outcomes in relation to both local contexts and national expectations. This emphasised the need to balance the interests of students with national policies and opportunities, and to consider whether the school works equally effectively for all of its students. Seeking out evidence to support their analyses of outcomes, groups of staff were able to use this to identify gaps and concerns that will become areas of focus, guiding their improvement efforts. They could then look specifically at ways in which teaching and leadership practices needed to be modified or developed within the school in order to enable the improvements to have impact. In evaluating this impact, they begin the next cycle of analysis for improvement priorities.

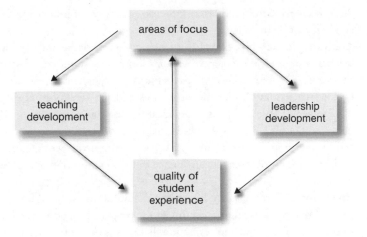

Figure 2.1 The IQEA framework

In using the IQEA model, schools were required to carry out a detailed analysis of their relative strengths and weaknesses in relation to their development priorities. Working together within a network, such analyses could be used to develop a shared understanding of strengths and weaknesses in relation to local contexts. One aspect of this involved the use of statistical data systems in conjunction with internal, inquiry-based approaches that generate qualitative evidence of learner experience and school performance. We found that such evidence often generated important questions, whilst at the same time challenging practitioners to reconsider their current ways of working, both as teachers and as leaders.

Examples of inquiry-based approaches that were found to be useful included the following:

1. **Analysing teaching.** This involved the use of evidence gathered through mutual observation, the analysis of video recordings and evidence collected from students. A powerful strategy here is 'lesson study', a systematic procedure for the development of teaching that is well established in Japan, Hong Kong and several other Asian countries (Hiebert, Gallimore and Stigler, 2002; Lo, Yan and Pakey, 2005). It involves staff from a group of schools working in threes to strengthen teaching and learning. Each trio chooses and plans one lesson — known as the 'research lesson' — that they will each teach. The aim is to share expertise as to how to involve all members of the class. As each member of staff teaches the lesson, their two colleagues observe the process, focusing specifically on the way stu-

dents respond. After each lesson the trio plan ways of improving the lesson before it is taught again.

2. **Analysing leadership.** Developing new and sustainable practices among teachers can rarely be achieved without some corresponding adjustments to organisational structures and procedures. This, inevitably, raises parallel questions regarding leadership structures and practice, both at the middle and senior levels. This is a practical process, since research in IQEA network schools led us to conclude that the most effective forms of leadership development are likely to be based within the workplace, using social learning processes that influence thinking and action in a particular context.

3. **Analysing differences.** We had many examples that showed how, under certain conditions, written accounts of the practice in schools can be used to stimulate discussion and reflection that makes use of the different ways of working that exist. These experiences also showed that joint visits to other schools in order to produce such accounts can have especially powerful effects. In this way, colleagues within a network were seen as sources of mutual challenge and support, bringing their own experiences and perspectives to the discussions that take place. Inevitably such activities tended also to stimulate reflection from the visitors on their own schools and practices.

4. **Analysing learner experiences.** Evidence of how students see their experience of school can be a powerful stimulus for change. However, our experience was that few schools have effective procedures for collecting authentic evidence from learners. On the other hand, successful head teachers tend to emphasise the time and effort they and their senior colleagues make in order to engage with groups of students, formally and informally, in order to appreciate their perspectives on school life (West, Ainscow and Stanford, 2005). Often such heads argue that it is through direct engagement with students and their concerns that provides them with insights into high leverage strategies for improvement. This being the case, we worked with schools to develop a range of effective strategies for collecting the views of students.

5. **Analysing community contexts.** Effective improvement requires those in schools to have an understanding of the communities they serve. Furthermore, progress in improving behaviour and learning is likely to be limited if the school has a poor image externally. The evidence is that head teachers who are successful in moving schools forward focus on analysing and changing both internal arrangements and the external image of their organisations (West, Ainscow and Stanford, 2005). Shifting reputations within a community is difficult to do, but it is essential to longer-term,

sustainable improvement. In particular, efforts have to be made to strengthen the social capital within the school by developing positive views towards education amongst families.

Our monitoring of developments in the schools involved in IQEA led us to conclude that such inquiry-based analyses can be a powerful means of stimulating schools' deliberations as they design their own improvement strategies. We also found that they were useful in identifying strategies appropriate to each school's own stage of development. In the case of schools that are relatively low performing, the initial emphasis was usually placed on gathering evidence that could be used to strengthen systems and procedures, through the tightening of management and leadership arrangements. For schools that are performing more effectively, the focus was likely to be on continuing improvement, not least by looking at within-school variation. We also found that there is always scope for the strengthening of teachers' classroom practices, as no school works equally well for all of its students. These findings from IQEA about the potential of inquiry-based approaches and the concern with the progress of all students led to the development of another project involving a network of schools.

An inclusion network

In 2000 we were members of a group of researchers who won a grant from the ESRC Teaching and Learning Research Programme that enabled us to push forward our ideas about inquiry-based approaches to the development of equitable schools and schooling. The initiative took the form of a three-year collaborative action research network, titled *Understanding and Developing Inclusive Practices in Schools*, and involved twenty-five urban schools, their associated three local education authorities and three universities (i.e. Canterbury Christ Church, Manchester and Newcastle). Together we explored ways of developing more inclusive practices in the schools through investigating the barriers experienced to such changes in the various contexts, and the methods used to overcome these barriers.

We embarked on this process with a good deal of practical experience about how to work with networks of schools, not least from over ten years of activity within IQEA. On the other hand, we set out with relatively weak theoretical foundations for the work. Much of what we did, therefore, was on a 'trial and error' basis, as we explored ways of engaging schools in issues around inclusion. By the end of the project, we were able to characterise the process as one of 'critical collaborative action research' (Macpherson *et al.*, 1998).

The multiple terms needed to label this process indicate its complexity and point to some of the tensions within it. The *action* strand of the project was embodied in a series of interventions that teachers undertook with a view to making their schools more inclusive. The starting point for these was workshops held within each of the three local authorities through which groups of teachers from each school began to think about barriers to learning and participation in their schools, and about what they might do to overcome these. The teacher groups then set about interventions in their schools. For the best part of three years they engaged in a cyclical process, whereby they changed an aspect of practice, monitored the outcomes of the change, reflected on what they had observed and made decisions about what to change next.

The *research* strand of the process took two forms. First, school teams were encouraged to investigate their own actions. Some began by carrying out an initial investigation of their current practice in order to inform their decisions about what to change. All of them, once they had embarked on action, were encouraged to collect evidence on the impact of that action in relation to school inclusiveness. Where necessary, the university research teams offered them technical support in this. Schools' ongoing decisions about the direction of change were, therefore, informed by the evidence they collected about impact. Second, there was a strand of meta-research, in which the university teams monitored and analysed the action research process in which school teams were engaged. This took the form of evidence from interviews and meetings in order to understand how the school teams conceptualised inclusion, used evidence to assess the inclusiveness of their schools, and set about making their schools more inclusive.

The *critical* strand of the process came from the engagement between university researchers and school teams around the issue of inclusion. The university teams took the position that inclusion was both a value which could be articulated with some degree of clarity, and a set of practices about which something was already known. Although the staff groups were encouraged to act flexibly in response to their own contexts, and to develop their own conceptualisations of inclusion within those contexts, the university researchers took it upon themselves to act as 'critical friends' in this process. Specifically, this meant that the university teams challenged their school partners about whether they had characterised the inclusiveness or otherwise of their current practice appropriately, and whether their proposed changes were likely to make their schools more inclusive.

The *collaborative* strand was, therefore, central to the process as a whole. School teams were dependent on university researchers to provide critical perspectives and technical support. More practically, they were dependent on them for the overall organisation and funding of the project. The university teams, on the other hand, were dependent on the school teams for the action strand of the project and for 'insider' information on what was involved in making schools more inclusive. Moreover, the school teams were the subjects of the 'meta-research' carried out by the university teams.

The form of the project, as we have described it, arose partly out of a set of explicit assumptions, grounded in both our own previous experiences and in the wider research literature. As we have explained, we had worked on development projects with groups of schools many times in the past, and knew something about what keeps schools engaged, and what produces change. The decision to invite schools to identify teams rather than lone project leaders, for instance, came from those earlier experiences. Likewise, as we indicated earlier, there is a long and productive history of action research reported in the scholarly literature. However, it is clear in retrospect that we added our own emphases and assumptions to this prior knowledge. For instance, although there is a literature on critical approaches to action research (Carr and Kemmis, 1986), we were faced with a particular challenge in respect to the theme of inclusion.

As we have explained, we saw inclusion as a value and set of practices about which something was already known. Moreover, as established authors and researchers in the field, we had played our part in generating this prior knowledge (e.g. Ainscow, 1999; Clark *et al.,*1999; Dyson and Millward, 2000). We also knew, from our own work and from others in this field that acceptance of the value and practices of inclusion were frequently resisted by practitioners who saw themselves as having other priorities and as working within constraints that made inclusive practice impossible. This was particularly the case in the then English policy context where a 'relentless focus on standards' was being imposed on schools by central government (Blair, 2005).

We therefore needed a means of releasing practitioners from the constraints of national policy and enabling them to change their value positions and assumptions. We saw the use of research evidence as offering this means. We made the assumption that, when practitioners were confronted by evidence about their own practices, they would – with appropriate encouragement from their critical friends – begin to recognise the non-inclusive elements of those practices and would find ways of making them more inclusive. Fortunately, this is what did happen most often.

What we noted as these developments occurred was neither the crushing of the schools' efforts to become more inclusive by the government's policies for raising standards, nor the rejection of the standards agenda in favour of a radical, inclusive alternative (Ainscow, Booth and Dyson, 2006a). In most of the schools, the two agendas remained intertwined. Indeed, the focus on attainment appeared to prompt some teachers to examine issues in relation to the achievements and participation of hitherto marginalised groups that they had previously overlooked. Likewise, the concern with inclusion tended to shape the way the school responded to the imperative to raise standards.

In trying to make sense of the relationship between external imperatives and the processes of change in these schools, we drew on the ideas of Wenger (1999) to reveal how external agendas were mediated by the norms and values within the schools, and how they become part of a dialogue whose outcomes can be more rather than less inclusive. In this way, the role of national policy emerged from the study in something of a new light. This suggests that schools may be able to engage with what might appear to be unfavourable policy imperatives to produce outcomes that are by no means inevitably non-inclusive.

Our analysis revealed how social learning processes within schools influenced people's action and, indeed, the thinking that informed their actions (Ainscow *et al.*, 2003). Often this was stimulated by various forms of evidence that created a sense of interruption to existing ways of thinking and working. Particularly powerful techniques in this respect involved the use of mutual observation, sometimes through video recordings, and evidence collected from students about teaching and learning arrangements within a school. Under certain conditions such approaches provided *interruptions* that stimulated self-questioning, creativity and action. In so doing, they sometimes led to a reframing of perceived problems that, in turn, drew attention to overlooked possibilities for addressing barriers to participation and learning.

We concluded, however, that none of this provided a straightforward mechanism for the development of more inclusive practices. We found that any space for reflection that was created as a result of engaging with evidence may sometimes be filled according to conflicting agendas. Indeed, we documented detailed examples of how deeply-held beliefs within schools prevented the experimentation that is necessary in order to foster the development of more inclusive ways of working (Howes and Ainscow, 2006, Ainscow and Kaplan, 2005). This reminded us that it is easy for educational problems to be 'pathologised' as problems inherent in students.

All of this led us to argue that a methodology for developing inclusive practices must take account of the social processes of learning that go on within particular contexts. From our experience, this requires groups of stakeholders to look for a common agenda to guide their discussions of practice and, at much the same time, a series of struggles to establish ways of working that enable them to collect and find meaning in different types of information. The implication of all of this is that becoming more inclusive is a matter of thinking and talking, reviewing and refining practice, and making attempts to develop a more inclusive culture.

Within the inclusion network, a key strategy emerged for encouraging this possibility through the development of a programme of school-to-school visits. These visits were not, however, always successful. This seemed to be particularly so when the host teachers interpreted the visits solely as opportunities for the visitors to learn. On these occasions, the hosts positioned themselves as teachers rather than learners. Typically, the visit then consisted of a demonstration or performance of various teaching strategies that had been judged to be successful. On these occasions, those receiving the visit might have merely rehearsed what they already knew and responded to questions beyond the procedural as if they were challenges, rather than openings for debate.

On the other hand, successful visits were usually characterised by a sense of mutual learning amongst hosts and visitors. It was noticeable, too, that the focus for these visits often took some time to identify and clarify. Indeed, the preliminary negotiations that took place were in themselves a key aspect of the process. So, for example, during one such visit, the visitors were each invited to observe two children. A simple observation framework focused on children's interactions with peers and teachers. Those to be observed were chosen by the class teacher on the basis that they were the children he knew least about in his class. In addition to observations, the visiting teachers were asked to interview the children. Again, a loose structure was devised but the main emphasis was on the visiting teachers following up things that they had seen during observations.

The personal nature of these observations, and the teachers' willingness to listen to feedback from colleagues from another school, drew our attention to the extent of the challenge that was sometimes involved in this sort of collaboration. Indeed, our experience was that such visits were not cosy, nor did they always result in a rosy glow.

In deriving lessons from these visits, we concluded that it was important to emphasise the variety of reasons why participants were able to frame the event as one from which everyone might learn. This was connected to the fact that the evidence that was generated, and the ways in which it was responded to, opened up further questions. The participants also had the time necessary, not just for the event itself, but for formulating the agenda for the visit and for quite lengthy discussion afterwards. Further, they had a wider forum – the network meetings – in which they felt comfortable enough to talk about quite 'risky' findings. In this forum they knew they had established the sorts of relationships where others were more likely to congratulate them on their work and be intrigued by what had happened, rather than to pass judgements.

The outcomes of the inclusion project have been widely reported in the scholarly literature (Ainscow, Booth and Dyson, 2004, 2006a, b; Dyson *et al.,* 2003; Howes *et al.,* 2004, 2005). In terms of the development of a methodology for enabling research to contribute to more equitable policy and practice, the main lessons we drew were as follows:

• It is possible to infuse a critical dimension into a collaborative action-research project, so that issues of social justice (in this case, a focus on inclusion) are considered as practitioners shape their action.

- The critical friendship of 'outsiders' (in this case, ourselves as researchers) is a way of keeping these issues on the agenda. However, equally (if not more powerful) is the role of outsider-researchers in enabling practitioners to collect and engage with evidence about their practice. Such engagement is capable of bringing about significant changes in practitioner thinking which is reflected in changes in practice.
- Where such changes take place, it is useful to think of them as the result of an 'interruption' to continuing practice which brings about a transformation from 'single-loop' to 'double-loop' learning (Argyris and Schon, 1978, 1996); that is, from learning which enables practice to be improved incrementally to learning which shifts the assumptions on which practice is based.

We also learnt more about some of the problems inherent in this way of working. For instance:

- Although transformations in thinking and practice occurred, they were far from universal. Some practitioners and their schools continued on their established course with little deviation.
- Although we understood 'inclusion' as a broad social justice issue, some practitioners interpreted it in rather narrow terms – for instance, as being about improving the attainments of low-attaining students. Because we did not offer practitioners a robust model of inclusion as a set of principles on which practice could be based, we were very much in the hands of teacher interpretations.
- In time, the research process generated a model of inclusive practice. However, this was at a very generalised level. It did not form the basis for any impact on policy, and was not readily transferable as it stood to other contexts.

Identifying common strands

These two projects clearly have much in common, not least in the way they:

- sought to stimulate a process of change in practice (i.e. they have an action strand)
- formulate action with reference to overarching principles
- have a research strand that invites practitioners to enquire into their own practice and assume that such inquiry will impact on the values on which practitioners act
- position university researchers as critical friends of and technical supporters for practitioners.

In drawing lessons from these and other similar experiences to inform sub-sequent projects, we sensed a need to provide a clearer framework for those taking part. In both the earlier projects, schools were issued with a rather open invitation to develop some aspect of their practice, and researchers tracked and supported their action in this respect. On reflection, we believed it would be helpful to offer a clearer initial specification of what would count as a more equitable state of affairs, in order for participants to review and develop their practices in the light of this specification.

We took the view that, organisationally, these initial specifications should be arrived at by working with a practitioner inquiry group. Once formulated, however, the specifications create a shared agenda within which all participants – practitioners and researchers – can talk to each other about their work, even when they are working on apparently separate issues in their own contexts. That same agenda then offers a means of identifying the sort of evidence that is needed – that is, information that will illuminate the current state of affairs in relation to the specification of a more equitable state. It also offers a means of identifying the sorts of outcomes that will make the project successful in participating sites – that is, new understandings and practices that move closer to the more equitable state of affairs – and that may lead to the development of 'models' that can be implemented elsewhere.

This led us to the view that our engagement in projects of the kind described here should be seen as a form of *development and research*. We did not embark on them with a predefined set of methods, nor yet with fully elaborated theo-retical propositions. We began rather with hunches, lessons from past experi-ence, and disparate theoretical resources. We were setting out to enable people with different assumptions, experiences and backgrounds, who happened to be engaged in the same sites of practice, to talk and debate together in order to develop sufficient shared understanding for them to be able to act in a coor-dinated manner. However, we were also seeking to create a situation in which any consensus at which they arrived could be problematised by the diversity of views and experiences within the group of actors, by the evidence about their practices which they collected, and by the provocations from researchers act-ing as critical friends. In this way, we anticipated that their shared 'single-loop learning' about 'how to do the same things better' would be complemented by 'double-loop learning', which questions the aims of and assumptions underpin-ning current practice.

A framework for development and research

Our subsequent work has taken the form of a series of collaborative projects with policy-makers and practitioners that are in some ways similar to IQEA and the inclusion network, building on what we learnt from those projects. In particular, where the earlier projects worked out their methods to some extent by trial and error, we now seek to found our current work on a robust and explicit methodology, which we characterise as development and research. At a practical level, this takes the form of a consistent series of questions which provide an organising framework for each project and which generate a series of steps through which the project proceeds. These are:

- **Situation analysis**
  What are the features of the situation under review? How do different stakeholders view that situation and what issues, problems and opportunities do they see within it? What evidence is there to support these different views?

- **Identification of priorities**
  What priority issues can be identified? What long-term aims and outcomes can be agreed? How can they be formulated in a way that is actionable?

- **Propositions**
  What has been learnt from approaches that have been tried previously? What does previous relevant research suggest as being useful starting points for action?

- **Theory of change**
  Can these propositions and priorities be formulated as a theory of change? Can this theory show what actions are needed, what changes will follow, and how these changes will lead to the desired outcomes?

- **Strategy**
  What resources are available for moving forward? How can they be mobilised? What constraints need to be taken into account? Who will do what?

- **Monitoring and learning**
  What forms of evidence will be collected in order to evaluate implementation, intermediate changes and longer-term outcomes? Who will collect and assess this evidence and what will be the roles of internal and external partners? How will learning from this process feed back into action?

These steps embody the practical knowledge we developed through our earlier work. They also articulate a clearer understanding of what would be the central focus of our work.

In the inclusion project, we were clear that we wished to understand something about the development of inclusive practices in schools. However, it was only as the project progressed that we came to understand that there were different types of knowledge about such practices. One was the knowledge that we as researchers possessed: about the meaning of inclusion, the practices that might realise inclusion, and the actions of practitioners in attempting to realise inclusive principles. Another was the knowledge and understanding that practitioners themselves had about these things – ranging from knowledge of 'what works here', to understandings of inclusion that might be very different from those that we held as researchers. Yet another was the knowledge that might be generated jointly by researchers and practitioners and made available to colleagues in other situations and at other times – in other words, generalisable and transferable knowledge.

We have, therefore, subsequently reconceptualised our work. We now see it explicitly as a process of knowledge-generation, occurring when researcher and practitioner knowledge meet in particular sites, and aimed at producing new knowledge about ways in which broad values might better be realised in future practice. This has implications for the relationship between researchers and practitioners. The critical relationship of their different kinds of knowledge has to be embodied in real encounters between these groups. This may involve close engagement, as in the sorts of networks we created in the two projects, or it may involve more distant encounters. In either event, it requires new forms of relationship between practitioners and researchers, in the way that is outlined helpfully by Hiebert, Gallimore and Stigler (2002). They suggest that fruitful forms of collaboration require a reorientation of values and goals amongst both groups. So, they argue, teachers need to move away from the dominant view that teaching is a 'personal and private activity'. Rather, teachers have to adopt the 'more risky view' that it is an activity that can be continuously improved, provided it is made public and examined openly. At the same time, they argue that researchers must stop undervaluing the knowledge teachers acquire in their own classrooms. In this way researchers will be able to recognise the potential of 'personal knowledge' as it becomes transformed into 'professional knowledge'.

Values and principles

Underpinning this conceptualisation is what we believe to be a clearer understanding of the significance of values and principles in our work. As we have explained, a feature of the two earlier projects was that both attempted to map these out, delineating the basis on which the partners would seek to work together. However, the significance of that values-base was somewhat underconceptualised. We tended to assume either that practitioners would share our values, simply because they opted into the project, or that we would find some means of 'converting' them to our views. What we learnt from these experiences was that neither of these assumptions was correct and, more particularly, that it makes little sense to separate out technical knowledge from the sets of values and assumptions in which such knowledge is embedded. So, for example, inclusion is neither a disembodied value nor a value-free set of practices, but rather an understanding about how to realise particular values in particular sites of practice (Artiles and Dyson, 2005).

It follows that we now see values as central to our engagement with policy-makers and practitioners. The initial 'situation analysis' in which we ask them to engage, therefore, is not an analysis of 'what is working' in their contexts, but an analysis of the extent to which particular values are actually being realised. This means that the learning which we seek to promote, the new knowledge which we seek to generate and the 'models' in which we seek to embody that knowledge are not merely technical in nature, but are about how values can be embodied in situated practices. The change process in which we engage with practitioners, moreover, is not simply a change in practice, but a change in the values which underpin practice and/or in understandings of how those values can be realised in particular situations. This is very different from – and, we suggest, much more challenging than – the technical developments that seem to characterise research and development approaches, or those action research approaches which focus only on practitioners exploring their practice within their own frames of reference.

At the same time, we now take the pursuit of more equitable educational provision – rather than school improvement or inclusion – as the underpinning emphasis within our work. This follows from our clarification of the role of values. We do not see our role as promoting a single, narrowly defined values position; much less to promote a particular set of practices that we see as embodying our preferred values. Rather, it is to reinforce broadly defined concerns to secure social justice in an education system that acknowledges such concerns, but, in our view, fails to act upon them adequately. From this perspective, it is helpful to be able to engage with practitioners and policy-makers in terms of some broad but explicit principles.

It follows that we have done a good deal of work in trying to map out our understandings of equity as an overarching concept which includes, but goes beyond inclusion (Ainscow *et al.*, 2009). The result is that we tend to agree with Braveman (2003) that equity is not a unitary concept that can be applied to all situations. Rather, we view it as an overarching – if somewhat generalised – value of 'fairness' or 'justice', which provides a series of lenses through which different situations can be examined.

This is consistent with the broad definition of equity used by the OECD, which focuses on two notions: 'fairness' and 'inclusion' (OECD, 2007: 11). Within this formulation, fairness is seen to exist where personal, social, economic and ethnic backgrounds do not present barriers to learners achieving their educational potential; and, inclusion exists where everyone is ensured a basic minimum standard of education. The OECD argues that the interconnected pursuit of fairness and inclusion can break the cycle of school failure and social disadvantage. These broad notions suggest looking at equity as a system-wide issue, not just one to be analysed at the individual school level.

So, we tend to ask whether the educational arrangements in particular situations are 'just', in terms of the real opportunities – 'capabilities' in Sen's terms (Fukuda-Parr, 2003, Sen, 2000) – that they offer learners for educational *access, participation and outcomes*. It is important to note that these lenses can be applied to the arrangements in which individual learners find themselves, but that we have a particular interest in the situation of socio-economically disadvantaged populations. We should also note that, in the English context, these populations include, but cannot be restricted to, different ethnic groups. Equity, therefore, may be an issue of race, religion or ethnicity, but it is not restricted to these.

Conclusion

Whilst much of the work of the projects described in this chapter has been clearly focused on within-school factors, we also saw how the involvement of schools in networks opened up possibilities for productive interactions between schools. Our experience over the years of working with such networks suggests to us that collaboration between schools is a practice that can both transfer existing knowledge and, more importantly, generate context-specific new knowledge regarding ways of teaching all children and young people effectively.

Together, these studies point to a series of conditions that seem necessary in order to make collaboration effective for the various partners. In summary, these are: the presence of incentives that encourage key stakeholders to explore the possibility that collaboration will be in their own interests; the development of a sense of collective responsibility for bringing about improvements in all the partner organisations; head teachers and other senior staff in schools who are willing and able to drive collaboration forward; the identification of common improvement priorities that are seen to be relevant to a wide range of stakeholders; the use of data as a catalyst for change; external help from credible consultants who also have the disposition and confidence to learn alongside their school-based partners.

In the absence of such conditions, attempts to encourage teachers and schools to work together are likely to result in little more than time-consuming meetings, which sooner or later will be seen as ineffective and discontinued.

Strategies for developing these conditions are, therefore, an important determinant of the success of school networks, which implies that they will need to be brought together and, indeed, held together by common purposes. What this might involve became an early focus for our interest in the Stockborough Equity Research Network, the project we now go on to describe.

3 The development of an equity research network

Bearing in mind the formulations described in the previous chapter, in what follows we describe the development of the Stockborough Equity Research Network (SERN) over a period of five years. We start by explaining how the network was set up and how it evolved, before describing the model of working that emerged and the organisational conditions that helped to facilitate its use.

In the final section of the chapter we begin to consider the extent to which the work that developed within and between schools moved towards system reform in relation to equity. As we will show in later chapters, the work of this network throws light on some of the difficulties we face in trying to foster greater equity in the current English policy context. In so doing, it draws attention to what needs to be done to develop more equitable education systems, both in our own country and elsewhere.

The context

The project was located in 'Stockborough', a district characterised by socio-economic disadvantage, and social and ethnic segregation. At the heart of the district is a town of around 82,000 people that was once a prosperous textiles centre. Most of the old industries have now disappeared, however, and unemployment is high.

The Victorian terraced housing near the centre of the town is mainly inhabited by British Asian families, whilst relatively poor white families live in areas of 1950s public housing estates on the outskirts. Some of these estates are characterised by the most extreme disadvantage in the country. Meanwhile, pockets of rejuvenated and gentrified housing are inhabited by mainly British white professionals working in the nearby cities.

At the start of the project, in 2006, the district's secondary school system comprised a hierarchy of sixteen schools, some selective on the basis of attainment or religious faith, with others being non-selective and described as comprehensive schools. There was also one secondary special school. Two of the comprehensive schools had no provision for 16- to 19-year-olds (usually referred to in England as sixth forms).

In terms of students' national exam results, the performance of these schools varied considerably. One of the schools was among the lowest performing schools in England, while the two selective schools were amongst the highest. Ten of the schools – including the ones at either end of the performance spectrum – were within a four to five mile radius of each other. There had been much emigration from the town. Indeed the local authority had 'failed' a government inspection in 1999, and the flight from the town was pinpointed as a key factor.

Setting up the network

There have been extensive efforts in recent years to encourage greater cooperation between schools. In particular, various government initiatives – such as Excellence in Cities, Networked Learning Communities, the Leadership Incentive Grant and City Challenge – have provided financial incentives for such arrangements, although these have usually proved to be temporary (Ainscow and West, 2006). A collaborative arrangement that had endured, however, was a network of four secondary schools in Stockborough that had existed for some eight years. However, whilst the head teachers had developed very good working relationships, and this had led to some collaborative activities, they felt that the impact had been limited. Consequently, they decided that there was a need to develop ways of working that would challenge practices, assumptions and beliefs of staff and governors, and which would help to create a stimulus for further sustainable improvement. With this in mind, they approached us to support and facilitate the use of research to strengthen their network. The schools agreed to fund our involvement.

We have given the schools the following pseudonyms: Central, Highlands, Moorside and Valley. One of the schools, Valley, served, in the main, a relatively affluent community and was perceived to be successful in terms of examination results; the other three served disadvantaged communities and had differing degrees of success. Two of the schools, Highlands and Moorside, were seen as being particularly unsuccessful and, therefore, struggled to enrol students. As a result, they were more likely to admit young people from less supportive families, students who had been excluded from other schools because of difficult behaviour, and others who arrived from outside the country, including refugees and asylum seekers.

With respect to the government's performance league tables, within Stockborough the schools were placed as follows out of the eleven non-selective comprehensive schools (A*–C refers here to the higher grades in the national GCSE examinations taken by most young people at age 15+).

Table 3.1   Rank of SERN comprehensive schools in performance league table for Stockborough

	Valley	Central	Highlands	Moorside
Attainment, taking into account government designed contextual indicators	9th	1st	3rd	11th
National attainment scores of 5 A*–C for 15 year-olds	5th	7th	10th	11th
National attainment scores of 5 A*–C for 15 year-olds including Maths and English	3rd	9th	10th	11th

During the first year of the network, one of the schools, Moorside, was put into 'Special Measures' as a consequence of an Ofsted inspection that found that it was failing to provide an acceptable standard of education. The inspectors had also concluded that the school did not have the capacity to improve. This situation had been exacerbated by the national media interest in the school. Ten years previously the school had been temporarily closed due to poor teaching and learning, unruly student behaviour and disaffected teaching staff. Since then it had been the focus of various government interventions before being put back in Special Measures.

Designing the project

In designing the project we took account of the organising framework for development and research projects outlined in the previous chapter. Based on lessons from our earlier projects, this took the form of questions used for planning purposes (as outlined in Chapter 2 under 'A framework for development and research'). Through discussions involving the four head teachers and representatives from the university, it was agreed that equity was a central issue facing each of the partner schools and that the project would be known as the Stockborough Equity Research Network (SERN).

Through these initial planning discussions it soon became evident that what the term equity meant was different in each of the four contexts, not least in respect to the groups of learners who seemed to be missing out within the existing arrangement. As a result, it was agreed that the work of the network should take account of these differences by adopting a broad set of research questions to focus its activities, within which each school would determine its own particular focus. These questions were as follows:

- Which of our learners are most vulnerable to underachievement, marginalisation or exclusion?
- What changes in policy and practice need to be made in order to reach out to these students?

- How can these changes be introduced effectively and evaluated in respect to student outcomes?

After the decision was made to establish SERN, members of our university team visited each of the schools to discuss in greater detail the sorts of issues that needed to be addressed and the organisational arrangements that were to be created to coordinate the project.

We took the strategic decision that participating schools should be asked to focus attention on groups of learners thought to be missing out within existing arrangements. Initially, we were anxious that this might lead to narrowly focused efforts to 'fix' students seen as being in some sense inadequate. As we explain in the following chapters, however, collecting evidence about these groups usually led to a re-focusing of attention around contextual factors that were acting as barriers to their participation and learning. In this way, most of the projects carried out gradually became mainstream school improvement efforts that had the potential to benefit many students.

Staff inquiry groups

Staff inquiry groups were set up in each school, consisting of five or six members representing different perspectives within their school communities. These groups took part in a residential workshop at which we discussed with them an initial analysis we had made of the area, based on a consideration of various documents, statistics and interviews with a selection of stakeholders, including head teachers, local authority staff, community group representatives and politicians.

We explained that our impression was of an area characterised by various forms of segregation, with the population divided by ethnicity and class, with these divisions being reflected in schools, and then being exacerbated by the existence of a selective system and the uneven distribution of sixth forms. We argued that, for us, this situation gave rise to a series of observations that seemed to be relevant to our equity focus:

- There had been a history of schools opting out of local authority control, mainly under the threat of a reorganisation of sixth form provision. Although this option had ended in 1999, some heads were still suspicious of the local authority.
- Because of the number of foundation schools (i.e. state schools that are semi-independent of the local authority, particularly in respect to their funding), 45 per cent of the workforce was not now employed contractually by the local authority.

- The tradition of transporting children from more distant areas to create ethnically mixed schools was now not possible since the council could no longer interfere with processes of parental choice.
- In 1996, when the current director of Children's Services came to the authority, education was seen as a major area of concern. During that same year one school had hit the national headlines and continued to attract national attention, making management of the situation difficult.
- There were particular cultural problems in the central area of the borough, including: the apparently inward-looking nature of the community; the lack of personal and social skills which even some graduates from the area had and which prevented them accessing employment opportunities; a possible under-reporting of child protection issues because of cultural perceptions of acceptable parenting; high rates of teenage pregnancy associated with young marriages; and a drugs culture in the area that offered alternative employment opportunities.

We explained that senior officers in the local authority had told us that they were adamant that Stockborough was manageable, although it had to be accepted that schools were diverse and, to varying degrees, autonomous. In this situation, however, the officers accepted that it was difficult for the authority – or any other body – to guarantee equity of educational provision.

This analysis led to some heated debate amongst the staff present at the workshop, as they reflected on what this meant for their own schools. At the same time, this added further information into our continuing efforts to make sense of the complexity of the context in which we were working.

Following this process of contextual analysis, we took the staff teams through a process of planning the investigations they intended to carry out. In so doing, we helped them to develop a clearer focus and plan the procedures they would follow. Subsequently, each school team set out to gather evidence about students identified as losing out in some way, the aim being to develop better insights regarding their experiences in the schools. The groups also shared their findings with their colleagues in the partner schools. In these ways, the intention was to deepen understandings of practices, beliefs, assumptions and organisational processes, both within and across the schools in the network.

School processes

As we have explained, our close monitoring of what happened in some of our earlier projects had revealed how social learning processes within schools influence people's action and, indeed, the thinking that inform their actions. We had also found that often this was stimulated by various forms of evidence that created a sense of interruption to existing ways of thinking and working. In so doing, this sometimes led to a reframing of perceived problems that, in turn, drew attention to overlooked possibilities for addressing barriers to participation and learning. However, as we have noted, none of this necessarily provides a mechanism for the development of more inclusive practices, since the space for reflection created as a result of engaging with evidence may be filled according to conflicting agendas.

In line with our development and research approach, then, we worked with the school teams on site, challenging staff interpretations and encouraging them to think through the wider implications of their work. Occasionally, the teams from the participating schools came together to report progress and interrogate each other's work and, gradually, this process became cyclical. (Figures 3.1 and 3.2 are examples of the posters prepared by inquiry teams to display their ideas.)

After one year, the schools committed themselves to a further year of involvement and to take action to involve other schools. In this way the intention was that all schools in the local district would become involved, on the assumption that equity requires coordinated community-wide action.

As we had proposed, developments during the first year in the four schools focused on particular groups of 'marginalised' students (see Table 3.2). Many of these groups were not the subject of existing school or national policy concern, and their identification suggested that many equity issues remain largely invisible in schools.

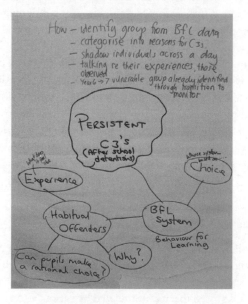

Figure 3.1 Poster prepared by the Valley team

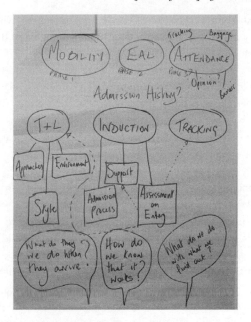

Figure 3.2 Poster prepared by the Highlands team

Table 3.2 Areas of focus in the four schools

Central	Underachievement	Many middle-ability students see themselves as educational failures, but still have high aspirations for work after school. Many drop out of post-16 education.
Highlands	Mobility	A significant number of students join the school between the ages of 11–16 and often in the middle of school terms.
Valley	Invisibility	A significant number of students have been identified as going unnoticed because they do not attract attention to themselves as either outstanding or challenging. They have been identified across the ability range.
Moorside	Attendance	18% of students do not attend and many more officially attend but do not go to certain lessons.

With our support, a set of appropriate tools to structure the generation of data was developed. These included an observation schedule focused on the experience of students identified as being marginalised in some way and a method for conducting student focus groups. These tools were chosen separately by school teams and adapted to varying degrees to suit the needs of each of their inquiries. At the same time, they were helpful in providing the basis of a contextualised common language – within and between the school inquiry groups – about the processes involved in their projects, and issues related to inequity in and across the schools.

The observation schedule comprised a set of criteria under broad categories related to different types of interactions of students in classrooms, namely, student–teacher relationship, questioning and answering, the tasks and the student, and the student and their peers. The focus groups revolved around asking small groups of students to identify and talk about learning experiences where they have felt involved and engaged in learning, and, conversely, activities where they have not felt involved or engaged in learning. They were then asked to expand on these, and also asked to discuss issues around fairness and being listened to.

The intervention strategies that school teams discussed to move their practice forward in more equitable directions ranged from building on and challenging current teaching and learning practices, to reconsidering school-wide systems, such as admissions procedures, and challenging the division of students into rigidly defined high, middle and low ability strands.

In general, we found that the school teams found the gathering of and engaging with data around the student experience to be a powerful stimulus for reflection, and, more importantly, to act as such at the level of management and whole school meetings. To this end, strategies involving more staff in gathering and engaging with more evidence about current practice were increasingly discussed.

Towards the end of the first year of the network, each school team was assisted by one of our university team in producing a collaborative account of their inquiry-based developments. These were then reported at a one-day conference for the four teams. It was intended that this process would deepen understandings of the issues of equity being experienced across their schools and, in so doing, encourage them to work more closely together to tackle inequities that went beyond the boundaries of their individual school walls. It was, however, unclear at this stage as to what this collaboration might involve. Although exploratory in style, at this early stage the project was guided by the broad proposition that greater educational equity is more likely to develop when school staffs' capacities to respond have been developed through collaborative practitioner-led inquiries.

Alongside materials and notes generated through the process of working with the network, we took part and observed meetings and other events in the schools. We also carried out semi-structured interviews and focus groups with those involved in order to generate evidence of what equity in education meant for them and their schools, how they felt it could be improved, the conditions that helped or hindered this, and the role the inquiries and the network had to play.

In these ways, we saw how evidence can challenge staff understanding of the barriers experienced by some of their students. In all four schools, marked shifts became evident – at both the individual and team levels – as evidence contradicted and elaborated prior understandings and taken-for-granted assumptions. We also observed how the staff teams sometimes encountered opposition from colleagues who refused to accept the meaning of the evidence they had generated. In such contexts, evidence generated from student 'voice' proved to be particularly powerful in challenging established meanings.

It was significant that, in each case, the relatively narrow initial focus widened as a result of the process and the schools began to address more fundamental issues of school improvement and equity. Our impression was that the extent to which this happened was shaped significantly by the willingness of school leaders to allow these issues to be explored; and by the wider culture of the school. Each team found ways of developing their practices in response to the process. However, external policy constraints opened some channels of development whilst closing many others.

Building up the network

The first year of SERN was, in many senses, very encouraging. It demonstrated the potential of a group of schools to work together, using various kinds of evidence to challenge inequities within their organisational contexts. At the same time, local historical factors continued to limit the impact of their efforts. In particular, trends within the 'market place' of the local education system continued to make two of the partner schools (Moorside and Highlands) extremely vulnerable, so much so that it was anticipated that Moorside would probably have to be closed. Meanwhile, head teachers in some of the other local schools expressed an interest in joining the network, even though there were intense pressures on all of the schools to look after their own individual interests.

Over the following four years SERN grew, such that by 2011 fourteen of the sixteen secondary schools in the local authority had been actively involved at one stage or another (Table 3.3 summarises the schools and their pattern of involvement in the network). Each paid an annual fee to the university for their involvement, although in some cases schools were able to secure funding from various national initiatives to cover these costs. Nevertheless, the willingness of the heads to pay to be involved was, in itself, an indicator of their commitment to make the network work for their schools.

During the five-year period, the work of the network was discussed regularly at meetings of the Stockborough Association of Secondary Head Teachers. In addition, each year a conference was held during which the staff inquiry groups presented the work they had been doing to colleagues from other schools and

Table 3.3 The schools involved in SERN

School name	Age range/numbers on joining the network	Dates of participation
Valley High	11–18 1,290 (2008)	2006–10
Highlands High	11–16 423 (2006)	2006–10
Moorside High	11–18 531 (2006)	2006–9
Central High	11–16 720 (2007)	2006–11
Westbury High	11–18 840 (2008)	2007–8, 2010-11
Castle High	11–19 123 (2008)	2007–11
South Dale High	11–18 1,644 (2008)	2007–9
Long Road Church of England High	11–18 988 (2009)	2008–10
Leafy Top High	11–18 1,235 (2007)	2008–10
Our Lady's Roman Catholic High	11–18 794 (2011)	2009–11
East Town High	11–18 1,430 (2010)	2009–10
Westlands High	11–18 1,441 (2008)	2010–11
Greenside Grammar	11–18 1,041 (2011)	2010–11
Outwood High	11–18 742 (2010)	2010–11

representatives of the local authority. In these ways, the development and research carried out in the participating schools continued to influence wider discussions across the local authority.

Meanwhile, over the same period changes occurred in national policy that had an impact on the work of the network. These changes were reflected in local developments, including the decision to close one of the founding schools, the announcement that another school would be replaced by an academy, and the designation of another school as being part of the National Challenge (a government initiative imposed on schools that had low scores in examinations). In this latter case, additional support was provided by the school becoming a federation with another school. It was significant, too, that during this period of extensive policy turbulence – nationally and locally – ten of the Stockborough head teachers left their posts (some of these were successive heads from one school), and in some cases were replaced by acting heads for up to a year.

At the end of the fourth year, funding became problematic for the whole network, partly because of the national and global recession, partly because the money from various national initiatives was running out, and partly because it was felt that the project needed to be coordinated more locally if it was to be sustained appropriately. Nevertheless, the head teachers and the teams from the schools made it very clear that they wanted the network to continue and for the university to remain a partner. In general, they argued that we acted as a neutral guardian and yet a critical friend, provided status, and stimulated knowledge growth and skills about schools, equity and ways of carrying out collaborative inquiries.

As in the first year, during subsequent years school teams investigated issues of equity. Sometimes the theme remained the same over two years, and sometimes a different issue emerged. As noted earlier, these issues were initially focused on a group of learners identified as vulnerable in some way. Examples of issues addressed by schools included students who:

- were described as being overlooked – variously referred to as 'grey', 'invisible', 'wallpaper' or 'ghost' students
- changed school after the normal starting times
- had English as an additional language
- were newly arrived in England
- had poor attendance and challenging behaviour
- dropped out of school
- had low aspirations
- came from disadvantaged families
- were persistently being punished through detentions
- were difficult to engage.

Whilst these areas of focus were varied, similar patterns continued to be evident in the ways that the inquiry groups conducted their work. Usually, the evidence gathered and discussions around it, led to unexpected insights and significant shifts in assumptions of the staff about the nature of the inequities or vulnerabilities associated with these groups of students. These findings then tended to prompt the teams to gather further evidence from different sources to explore the situation more deeply, and to work together to makes sense of the evidence. In many cases, this led to more surprises and shifts in assumptions, often leading to a level of dissatisfaction about what was happening around the students and a sense of responsibility to do something about the situation. The collective experience of making sense of the evidence also seemed to provide a space where team members could talk openly and reflectively with colleagues in different roles who they would not otherwise have the opportunity to talk to in such a way. In general, as in the first year, the process involved moving away from explanations based on the characteristics of the young people themselves, towards an exploration of contextual factors, such as the curriculum, teaching practices, attitudes and relationships that appeared to bear on the experiences of these learners.

Usually, the teams went on to share their evidence with their colleagues at department or whole-school meetings. To varying degrees these challenged and stimulated thinking, and in some instances caused a degree of discomfort. Some of the investigations led on to tangible developments in practices in the schools. These included embedding mutual observations between groups of three staff members in the school year, to making procedural changes to admissions of new students starting outside the normal starting time, to more subtle individual changes relating to how the staff interacted with students in class. However, some schools did not introduce explicit changes and, in a few instances, the changes that were made were not monitored systematically, despite our advice that this would be helpful.

As a consequence of the experience of investigating students' experiences, and, in particular, recognising the power of listening to the views of young people, some staff groups became keen to involve their students more actively in the inquiry process. As a result, from the end of the second year onwards, we introduced occasional workshops on research methods for groups of students so that they, too, could carry out their own inquiries.

The SERN model

Gradually, as SERN developed, a model of working was refined, such that new schools that joined could be given a fast-track induction. The presence of staff members in existing schools who had developed a deep understanding of the processes involved and the actions needed to put them into practice – and who could, therefore, give authentic accounts of what they had done – was also helpful in this respect.

In support of efforts to introduce new schools to the SERN approach – or, indeed, new colleagues within existing schools – a guide was developed. This document explained the rationale and presented a planning framework to assist schools in developing, implementing and evaluating strategies for addressing equity. All of this was related to the overall agenda of SERN, which had eventually been amended, as follows:

•   Which learners are most vulnerable to marginalisation or exclusion or underachievement in our schools?
•   What is the quality of their experiences in school?
•   What changes are needed to reach out to these students?
•   How can these changes be developed effectively and monitored with respect to students' lived experiences?

The guide stressed that the aim was to address this agenda within each of the participating schools but also across Stockborough. It argued that research suggests that such an approach – involving networking between schools – has the potential to strengthen the overall impact. In other words, we were promoting the ideas that each school should make greater progress because they were working within a network that is itself more geared to innovation.

The rationale and suggestions presented in the guide were based on lessons from our earlier projects and the experience of the four schools that took part in year one of SERN. They were built around the following propositions:

1. **Schools know more than they use**. Thus the main thrust of development has to be with making better use of existing expertise and creativity within each school, and across the network.
2. **The expertise of school staff is largely unarticulated**. Therefore, in order to access the reservoir of unused expertise, it is necessary to create a common language of practice through sharing the detail of practice that will facilitate mutual reflection and the sharing of ideas.
3. **Evidence is the engine for change**. Specifically, evidence of various forms can help to create space for re-appraisal and rethinking by interrupting existing ways of thinking, by involving others, and by focusing attention on overlooked possibilities for moving practice forward.
4. **Working together is socially complex.** Successful networking requires new thinking and, indeed, new relationships that create active connections amongst partners within and across schools.
5. **Working together creates relationships that make things happen**. More specifically, arrangements need to be made that encourage the trust, mutual understanding and shared values and behaviours that will bind individual and school members of the network together and make openness, risk-taking and cooperative action possible.

In taking the project forward, it was suggested in the guide that schools would need to take the following actions:

• Select inquiry teams of five to six members. These people need to have the capacity to drive developments forward, provide a variety of perspectives, and have a willingness to see difference as an opportunity for critical reflection and change.
• Conduct inquiry-based developments within and between the schools, involving students as well as staff.
• Participate in and contribute to cross-school meetings and events.
• Incorporate the inquiry-based developments into the school development plan.
• Engage the rest of their school staff in their inquiries, through workshops, training days or other school meetings.

The work of the school groups was to be guided by the SERN planning framework (see Figure 3.3).

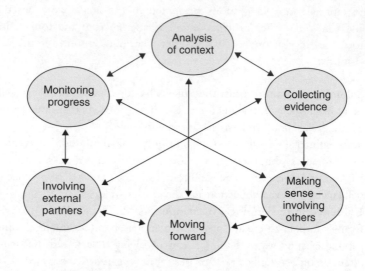

Figure 3.3 The SERN planning framework

As can be seen, the planning framework consists of six interlinked elements, each with its own set of issues for consideration. These elements were explained in the guide as follows:

1. **Analysing our context.** In order to develop effective strategies for reaching learners who are vulnerable to underachievement, marginalisation or exclusion there is a need to analyse the contexts within the school and the community. In this way, initial 'hunches' can be developed as to the sorts of barriers experienced by these learners and what actions might need to be taken to acknowledge these experiences and to overcome them. This is why it is helpful to have members of the inquiry team who have different perspectives on the life of the school.

Issues to consider:

*   Which groups of learners are missing out within our school?
*   What do we know about these groups?
*   Which group(s) should we focus attention on?
*   What are our hunches about the factors that lead to their marginalisation?

2. **Collecting evidence.** Building on initial hunches, arrangements need to be made to collect additional evidence of various forms to deepen the inquiry team's analysis. Here evidence can take many forms. It is likely to include statistical material that is readily available within the school, such as

attendance and performance data. This may point to individuals and groups for whom there is concern. In a sense, this gives a general picture of what is happening in the school in relation to these students. The next step involves a much more specific analysis of the situation, using qualitative data, including evidence provided by the students themselves. Research has found that such evidence can provide a powerful means of moving schools forward, not least because it may challenge the assumptions of staff as to why some students are vulnerable to marginalisation, exclusion and underachievement. It may also draw attention to students who are being overlooked.

Issues to consider:

- What further information do we need about the group of learners?
- How can we collect, record and analyse this information?
- Who needs to be involved?
- What forms of support do we need?

3. **Making sense of the evidence.** Having collected and considered various kinds of evidence, the inquiry team will need to plan ways of orchestrating a widespread discussion within their school community as to the issues that need to be considered. This is likely to involve placing the matter on the agendas of the senior management team, appropriate staff meetings, training days, the student council, governors and parent groups. Some schools have also found it useful to involve local authority support staff and representatives from their partner schools in these discussions, not least because 'outsiders' can helpfully ask questions and note patterns that 'insiders' are overlooking, and reflect on their own situation. In a sense, this is a way of *making the familiar unfamiliar* in order to encourage deeper processes of reflection within the school community. Where this is well-led, it is a means of drawing people together around a common sense of purpose. Research suggests that such involvement is the most effective means of encouraging school development. Clearly, the most important role of the inquiry group is to coordinate and stimulate the process. At the same time, it will be essential that members of the senior management team are seen to be actively involved.

Issues to consider:

- What does the evidence suggest about learners' experiences?
- What factors appear to be associated with their marginalisation?
- What does this tell us about our underlying assumptions?
- Who else needs to be involved in making sense of this evidence?
- What might we do to address these factors?

4. **Moving forward and involving others.** Having established areas for development, it will be necessary for the inquiry team to formulate strategies for involving the school community in moving forward. Here, as noted earlier, the overall approach is based on the assumption that *schools know more than they use* and that the logical starting point for development is with a detailed analysis of existing ways of working. This allows good practices to be identified and shared, whilst, at the same time, drawing attention to ways of working that may be creating barriers to the presence, participation and learning of some students. At this point it is helpful to remember the old adage, *school improvement is technically simple but socially complex*. In other words, planning the actions that are needed is likely to be relatively straight forward; the challenge for the team is to find ways of getting everybody involved. Inevitably, the actual strategies adopted will depend upon the nature of the areas being addressed.

Issues to consider:

• How do we need to change our inquiries in response to what we have found out?
• What action are we proposing to improve students' experiences?
• Who needs to be involved in order to move forward and how can we engage them?
• What actions do we need to take and how can we monitor them closely?

5. **Involving external partners.** The involvement of external partners will be important as the school moves forward in relation to its plans. There is considerable evidence that school-to-school collaboration can add value to the efforts of individual schools to develop more equitable ways of working. This shows how collaboration between schools can help to reduce the polarisation of schools, to benefit in particular those students who are marginalised at the edges of the system and whose performance and attitudes cause concern. There is evidence, too, that when schools seek to develop more collaborative ways of working, this can have an impact on how school staff perceive themselves and their work. Specifically, sharing and comparing practices can lead staff to view underachieving students in a new light. Rather than simply presenting problems that are assumed to be insurmountable, such students may be perceived as providing feedback on existing classroom and school arrangements as well as other service arrangements. In this way, students may be seen as sources of understanding of how these arrangements might be developed in ways that could be of benefit to all schools, and other community members. All of this has the potential to make an important contribution to the multi-agency work that

is now at the heart of the *Every Child Matters* policy agenda. Collaborating with partners external to school, such as community groups, businesses, other local authority services and agencies, is key to this.

Issues to consider:

- What are the factors about which we need to work with others from outside the school?
- Who do we need to work collaboratively with from outside the school?
- How can we get them involved?
- In what ways can we add value to each other's efforts?

6. **Monitoring progress.** This stage merges with 'analysing our context'. As the school moves forward with its plans it is necessary for the process of implementation to be carefully and frequently monitored. Evidence gathering of what is happening as developments progress will be needed. This is to determine their impact on the lived experiences of students and how to respond. Examples include informal comments made by staff or students, or video recordings of meetings or activities. Whilst the work of the inquiry team is key in coordinating this, senior and middle managers must also be involved in order to create an 'inquiring stance' throughout the school.

Issues to consider:

- What are the outcomes we are seeking?
- What do we expect to see happening in the process of achieving these outcomes?
- How do we monitor these actions and their impact on learners?
- How do we respond to their impact on learners and arrangements in school?

In the guide, it was explained that as the work of the staff team develops it is expected to have a wider impact in the school. In this way, it was anticipated that the initial focus on groups of learners seen as being 'at risk' was likely to challenge existing thinking and practices within the schools. This located the work of the network more centrally within the schools' overall development plans, and in relation to the plans of other local services and community groups in order to help support these developments across Stockborough.

It was explained that researchers from the university would provide support to schools as they used processes of inquiry to move thinking and practice forward. Specifically, this would involve us in:

- organising cross-school workshops for the inquiry teams in order to strengthen their skills in using evidence and sharing each other's experiences to drive improvement efforts;

- providing direct support to the schools in designing and carrying out their staff-led and student-led inquiries in relation to their school development agendas;
- coordinating cross-school activities in order to make better use of available expertise within the network;
- providing support in presenting ongoing findings to other school staff, students and services and community members;
- linking the network schools to relevant development and research activities nationally and internationally;
- meeting with the head teachers and link coordinators to explore strategic implications of the findings of the network's research activities (link coordinators were representatives from each staff team who coordinated in-school activities); and
- supporting the teams in writing accounts of these processes.

In addition, we explained that our task would be to analyse and document processes and outcomes of what happened in each school. In this way we aimed to produce detailed evaluative case studies that could be used to inform developments in other contexts, both in this country and internationally. In this sense, the project was to be seen as a process of collaborative critical action research, but one that would require change at all levels of the system. It would involve practitioners and academics working together to make use of the best available knowledge in order to develop more effective strategies for improving the quality of experience provided for all students.

Organisational arrangements

As the work of schools within SERN developed around the ideas outlined in the guide, so did the organisational arrangements used to support their activities. A crucial factor here was a programme of meetings with the head teachers. These occurred four to five times during each year, providing an important context within which we could discuss strategic matters related to the developments within the schools and the collaborative developments across the network. Schools took it in turn to host these meetings and, at each one, members of one of the staff inquiry teams gave a short account of their project. We saw, too, how these meetings provided the heads with opportunities to share concerns about the challenges they were facing more generally and offer advice to one other as to how these concerns might be addressed.

In addition, meetings of link coordinators were established in the third year of the project and took place five to six times a year. They were mostly senior leaders with access to resources and decision-making powers within their schools. At these meetings, decisions were made as to how to take the network forward, and issues debated regarding the theme of equity. Significantly, members of this group rejected our suggestion of a member of the local authority's educational support services joining the group since they were concerned that the network should not be taken over in ways that might lead to the imposition of externally driven agendas and performance targets. This tended to frustrate local authority staff, some of whom wanted to get involved in what they saw as a potentially important group.

Meanwhile, as in the first year, cross-school inquiry team meetings happened about five times a year. These were usually after-school events. Again, schools hosted the meetings and this provided informal opportunities for colleagues to learn about the work going on within the partner schools. During these events we gave short inputs to stimulate discussion about processes of school-based inquiry, orchestrated problem-solving discussions, and structured group activities that enabled the staff teams to learn from one another.

As we have explained, cross-school student workshops were introduced at the end of the second year. These were run two to three times a year and involved six or so 13- to 15-year-old students from each school. As with staff, the students were surprised to find how similar their issues of fairness were to their peers from other schools.

The annual SERN conference became an important event for the schools and, indeed, gradually became significant more widely within the local authority. By the third and fourth years, some 100 or so people attended, including senior leaders from other schools and senior children's services professionals working in the district. (Figure 3.4 shows one of the conferences.)

Figure 3.4 Presentations at a SERN annual conference

The aim was for the participating schools to share the issues they were facing and to work towards supporting one another in tackling these concerns. At times, presentations at these conferences veered towards 'showcasing'. However, over the years, experiences came to be described in a more authentic way.

In some cases, the teams used SERN events to express their dissatisfaction with what was going on in the local district. For example, at one stage Moorside High School's inquiries were about its imminent closure and the impact of this on students. Even though the school had improved its performance in the previous year, it was decided that the school had no future. Staff made a plea for the schools receiving students to take them early so that they might better settle in. They also asked colleagues to make sure that these students were treated with respect. On another occasion, staff from Castle, the special school, made a plea for better provision to be made for students with special needs leaving school at 19. They showed a video of parents talking about the negative experiences their young people had had after leaving school.

Developing roles

As the network developed, cooperation between the schools seemed to improve as a result of the coordination arrangements that were introduced. As this happened, we noted increased levels of trust and openness between representatives of the partner schools. We took all of this to be an indication of greater *social capital*, i.e. shared values and assumptions that, because they are commonly 'owned', are available for all members of a social community to draw on when transferring knowledge and understandings (Mulford, 2007).

Being prepared to reveal worries about your own school is potentially threatening within an education system that is so dominated by competition. In some cases, staff visited one another's schools in ways that drew back the veil of secrecy. At the same time, some of the groups began to learn the potential power of sharing data and using external colleagues as critical friends in relation to drawing out implications for further improvement efforts.

Sometimes, team members from other schools also provided support. For example, at one memorable whole-school meeting, some team members from the other schools came along to observe, to show support and act as critical friends. Staff from inside and outside the school found the experience extremely powerful not just in terms of providing support but as a way to hold a mirror up to each school's practices.

All of this points to one of the key challenges: that of finding time. In this respect, it became evident that where heads and senior staff experienced the benefits of collaboration, they were prepared to make strategic decisions to release human resources in order to invest in the strengthening of their partnerships. This reminds us that, as far as schools are concerned, time is the currency used to indicate that something is of importance. In other word, there is no extra time but if we see something as being a priority, we find the time. In this sense, attitudes and beliefs are important factors. It was noticeable, for example, that during the early stages the idea of working in a network was sometimes met with a degree of understandable cynicism. Indeed, in a few of the schools this was not fully overcome, particularly amongst senior staff.

Progress seemed to be associated with activities around agendas that were determined by schools and that were seen to have the potential to make direct contributions to the core business of teaching and learning. This seemed to create a common sense of purpose and, indeed, a common process for implementation that encouraged the sharing of expertise.

In monitoring these developments we saw evidence, too, of the key roles of individuals in providing leadership, maintaining the impetus and encouraging cooperative action within and between schools. In this context, progress seemed to be strongly associated with a sense of shared leadership, particularly amongst heads and other senior staff. Such an approach seemed to emerge over time, as relationships deepened and trust grew.

Despite the impressive progress that was made, however, the processes involved continued to be fraught with uncertainties, not least because of the absence of an overall policy direction – locally and nationally – that endorsed the agenda of the network and the processes used to address this agenda. Consequently, as we explain in subsequent chapters, its work remained fragile in ways that throw light on the way national policies, as they are interpreted at the local authority level, impact on the actions of schools.

System change

Throughout the period of the network we continued pushing the idea that those involved – particularly the heads – should see what was going on through a systems lens. In particular, we argued that efforts to achieve greater equity within individual schools would be limited in their impact if they were not part of a wider plan to create an education system that was based on notions of fairness and social justice.

With this argument in mind, in 2007 we prepared a discussion paper that suggested ways of strengthening the impact of SERN within the schools. In the paper we set out to what might be done in order to move the network forward. The paper argued:

> The initial focus on groups of students seen as being in some senses 'at risk' is gradually being seen as a challenge to existing practices within the

schools. This locates the work of the network more centrally within the schools' overall development plans. In so doing, it points to the need to refine the framework within which the network operates in order to focus more directly on practices of teaching and leadership, and the assumptions that inform these ways of working. It also draws attention to ways in which processes of collaboration within and between the schools might add value to the developments that are taking place.

The paper went on to suggest the use of the lesson study approach – referred to in the previous chapter – explaining that we had found this to be a powerful means of fostering professional development within and between schools.

The discussion amongst the heads that was provoked by the paper was rich and enthusiastic. In some instances, it helped in moving the agenda of SERN nearer to the central processes of development within the schools. On the other hand, the work of the network itself remained somewhat marginal to the ongoing discussions taking place amongst the wider Stockborough head teacher's association.

Meanwhile, we took part in what seemed to us like parallel discussions with local authority colleagues who took the decision to introduce a campaign to improve provision for children and young people in Stockborough. Despite the fact that the head teacher of one of the founding schools left his post to lead this initiative it remained largely disconnected from the ongoing work of the network in a way that left us somewhat baffled, to say the least.

All of this was brought to a head during the fourth year of SERN, as it became clear that the then Labour government was planning a further phase of reform that would encourage schools to become more autonomous. This move was signalled in the summer of 2009 with the publication of a White Paper on *The development of 21st Century school systems*, with its proposals that there should be a greater emphasis on schools supporting one another. From our perspective, this seemed to open up a potentially favourable policy environment within which to strengthen the school partnerships we had been developing. The key things, therefore, were to get agreement amongst the heads and to create a coordinating mechanism for developing a relevant strategy.

With all of this in mind, we put forward another discussion paper to the heads group in which we outlined what we described as 'two obvious possibilities' for moving forward in the new policy context:

Option 1. SERN could continue along the existing lines, with the university as a partner. As before, all secondary schools would be invited to join for the year. If this option was taken, it would seem sensible for overall coordination of the programme to be carried out locally, for example, a senior member of staff could be seconded to do this. The university group would concentrate on supporting development and research activities in the schools. Consequently, the financial contribution from schools would be less than in previous years.

Option 2. The SERN schools could set up their own local mechanism for coordination of further activities, without the involvement of the university. Overall leadership for this would be provided collectively by the head teachers, with a group of school representatives meeting occasionally to plan the programme of activities. A relatively small resource could be pooled to second one senior member of staff to coordinate the programme.

Discussion of these possibilities with some of the heads suggested a third, more radical option. This would involve an attempt to scale up the operation through the Stockborough association of secondary head teachers in a way that would involve all of the schools. Whilst equity would remain a central theme, the aim would be to use the experiences of SERN to create a new kind of cross-authority strategy for supporting school improvement more generally. Reflecting what seemed to be the direction of travel within national policy, this would involve the creation of an innovatory approach within which schools would look to one another for support: sharing expertise and working together to develop new responses, particularly in relation to vulnerable groups of learners. It was noted that, in a policy context where there was likely to be even greater diversity of provision – including more academies and, possibly, so-called free schools – a strong case could be made for such a collaboration. In particular, it offered a means of avoiding forms of fragmentation within the education system that would work to the disadvantage of certain groups of learners.

It was also noted that, within such a strategy, the presence of the university could be useful in terms of providing further knowledge, brokering the exchange of expertise, and branding the overall strategy. Accreditation of professional development through a customised Master's degree might be one means of funding this involvement. Such a strategy would also require a re-negotiation with the local authority regarding the role of its staff.

As it turned out, despite what seemed like a lot of interest in these suggestions, no actions emerged, apart from the fact that, as from September 2010, the former head of Long Road High was employed on a part-time basis to help coordinate the work of the network locally. Occasionally, over the next few months the topic did come up at various head teacher gatherings and, indeed, in discussion with local authority officers, but still without any practical outcomes. Meanwhile, the summer of 2010 saw another major change in national policy with the election of a new government

Conclusion

In this chapter we have described the development of SERN over the five years, showing its development from an initiative involving four schools to one that has involved almost all of the secondary schools in the borough. The account illustrates how the pioneering work of the founding schools built on and took forward the lessons of the projects described in Chapter 2.

We have explained how the inquiry-based approach was refined in the form of a guide that could be used with newcomers to the network. We have also summarised the organisational conditions that were gradually created in order to support the school inquiry teams in using the ideas outlined in the guide. Finally, the chapter has traced our unsuccessful efforts to encourage the schools to see the collaboration that had grown through SERN as the basis of a more fundamental strategy for continuing the process of system-level improvement.

In the following chapters we look more closely at what all of this meant for the development of the participating schools. As we will see, this offers reasons for optimism about the approach we were developing with our school partners, whilst, at the same time, further illuminating the difficulties involved in using the approach to bring about system-level change.

4 Making schools more equitable

As we explained in the previous chapter, the starting point each year for the work of SERN was an initial workshop, where the staff inquiry teams discussed their schools and fine-tuned their areas of focus. Based on their initial hunches, the teams went on to analyse their school contexts in terms of groups of students they regarded as marginalised in some way. At the same time, the teams speculated over possible reasons for these perceived vulnerabilities.

This approach of focusing on particular groups of students assumed to be in some sense at risk of marginalisation – or missing out – had emerged from our earlier discussions with the head teachers of the four founder schools. Right from the outset we had been troubled by this way of thinking, fearing that it appeared to assume a deficit view of these groups, perhaps, implying they had to be 'fixed' in order that they could take advantage of what their school was offering.

As we illustrate in this chapter, this concern proved to be largely unfounded. Rather, we saw how, through processes of inquiry, the school teams gradually moved their focus away from these groups of students towards factors within the context of the school. More specifically, we saw how the data the teams gathered and discussed led to unexpected insights and significant shifts in assumptions about the nature of the vulnerabilities associated with these students.

These initial findings tended to prompt the teams to gather more data from different sources to explore the situation more deeply, and to work together to make sense of the evidence. In many cases, this led to more surprises and shifts in assumptions, often leading to a level of dissatisfaction about what was happening around the students and a sense of responsibility to do something about these situations.

Drawing on the experiences of four of the schools, in what follows we illustrate how these processes led to rethinking amongst those involved. Whilst each of these accounts is distinctive, they all in their own way illustrate the pattern we have just summarised. At the same time, they begin to illustrate some of the difficulties of using this approach within current policy contexts.

Invisible students

Some of the school inquiries led to significant development in thinking and practice, usually as a result of surprising findings. The developments at Valley High were an example of this happening. One of the founder members of SERN, it is a comprehensive school for 11- to 18-year-olds, serving a diverse community, culturally and economically. Many of the students came from what might be described as alternative creative backgrounds, leading the head teacher to comment, it was '*the first time I'd seen young teenagers in a school sitting along the corridors busking on their guitars*'.

An assistant head explained that the school was '*the nearest you were going to get to a comprehensive in the area*', meaning that its population was diverse. He added that the parents of many of the children, for ideological reasons, chose to send their children to this non-selective school rather than one of the local grammar, faith or private schools. A minority of students came from socio-economically disadvantaged families, mainly living on a nearby public housing estate. In addition, there were twenty or so looked-after children, some of whom travelled across local authority boundaries to get to the school.

Many of the staff at Valley had been there for well over a decade. Although there was what seemed to be a comfortable air in the school, when a new head teacher joined the school, his immediate interpretation of this was that it was 'coasting'. In an attempt to develop a more consistent overall approach, one of the new policies he introduced was about 'behaviour for learning'. This was seen to have a significant impact on students, lessons and staff – although there were a variety of views as to whether this was positive or negative.

During the first year of SERN, a group of six staff was selected by an assistant head teacher to work with her. They set out to investigate students' allegiances and affinity with the school, as there was a sense that the majority left the school having had a 'slightly disappointing' time. The team had a hunch that the young people did not feel that they belonged to the school; instead, they either had strong allegiances to disparate teenage groups, or felt excluded from these groups. It seemed, too, that there might be a connection between this and a more general lack of interest in school amongst students. With this in mind, the team decided to identify learners in Year 9 who appeared to demonstrate this sense of disinterest in the recorded punishments and merits they received via the new behaviour system.

Looking at what had happened during the first weeks of term, the inquiry team was surprised to find that about 25 per cent of the students – with equal numbers of boys and girls – seemed to be 'invisible'. A teacher explained:

> We looked at the whole of our Year 9 and identified those with 100 per cent attendance. Sadly and rather surprisingly, we found that 25 per cent of these students had no detentions but also less than ten commendations for good work or effort, a tiny number in comparison to some students who had received over 100 commendations in the same period of time. It made us think very hard about how one quarter of our Year 9 students could effectively be going unnoticed during their time in school, and the implications of this on our exam results.

Even more surprising was that – contrary to expectations – these students were from across the ability range. As one member of the team explained:

> At our first meeting, we agreed that there was a group of young people at our school who we suspected were having a slightly disappointing time, developing little allegiance to it and simply going through the process from Year 7 to Year 11. We also realised we did not know much about this group of students, nor could we identify easily who they were. We had wrongly suspected that they were those grey GCSE grade C/D borderline kids who everybody said they were going to target but nobody ever did, because you were focusing on those who were going to get A*, A and B, and those who had special needs or other difficulties who needed additional support.

All of this led the staff team to change tack. Clearly, these young people were not being noticed in the classroom, either through their learning or their behaviour. Consequently, the team decided to investigate the experiences of the students more closely to see what this could tell them about practices within the school.

With this in mind, they observed the students in class to see what their experiences of learning and interactions were. The aim was to observe the lessons 'through the students' eyes'. A decision was made to concentrate on twelve students, six of each sex. With the help of one of the university team members an observation schedule was developed. This focused on four main areas: the interaction and relationship between the student and teacher; the interaction of the student with tasks set; the interaction of the student with peers; and the general disposition of the student.

Over a period of two weeks or so, members of the staff team observed each of the twelve students in at least two different lessons. Most of the team saw them in more lessons, since they found the process so interesting. Additionally, a researcher from the university observed some of the same students to see how, as an outsider, her observations differed from the team's. This was also intended to create the possibility for more meaningful discussion around the experience of the learners. The team then wrote reflective summaries about what they had found out.

Having emailed each other their summaries, the team met together to discuss what they had written and experienced. Ground rules were set from the start: in particular, it was decided that names of teachers would not be used, in order to avoid conversations around performance. Despite this, on some occasions staff names were mentioned during the conversations but the team still tried to respect the ethical position they had agreed.

Whilst there were minor differences in what was observed, the staff were struck by how similar the experiences of the students were. In particular, they noticed that their targeted students were rarely named or approached in class. Rather, they were seen to either work through their tasks quietly, often finishing before other students but not then demanding attention, or they were quietly off task, sometimes distracting other students. During whole class question and answer sessions they were generally unassertive in their body language, half of them hardly ever raising their hands or not responding at all.

Reflecting on these observations, a member of staff commented:

> We discussed our findings together and it was clear that we were all surprised by the similarity in these students' experiences and by the kind of experiences these students were having, many of which we too had overlooked. We also all found the experiences of observing students in different disciplines immensely refreshing in contrast to carrying out performance management observations in our own subjects. It was beneficial in terms of reflecting on our students' experiences of learning, our classroom practice and our perceptions of certain students.

As a consequence of these further surprises, the team decided to carry out focus group discussions with the students to find out what they had to say about their classroom experiences and the school more generally. Their hunches were that these students did not want to be noticed – that they were happy to not be the focus of attention in lessons. However, once again their assumptions were challenged by what the students said.

It was decided to mix the twelve students with twelve others, picked randomly from Year 9. This was so that these potentially more 'visible' students might help to develop a more dynamic and relaxed discussion, as well as providing insights into their experiences of learning. Two researchers from the university conducted the focus groups in order that the students might feel more able to express themselves. They were also mindful of who the target learners were so that they could make sure everyone's voice was heard.

During the focus groups the students were asked to identify and write down a recent learning experience where they had felt involved and engaged in learning, and, conversely, activities where they have not felt involved or engaged. They were asked to expand on these, and to also discuss issues around fairness and being listened to within the school. They were told that names of teachers or subjects would be removed, and that anything they said would be treated confidentially.

The students were all well able to articulate what they felt worked and did not work for them. They were also acutely and sometimes painfully aware that some students got more attention than they did. Among other things, they articulated their dislike for copying out texts, and their enjoyment of activities where they could think for themselves, as long as tasks were explained clearly and they 'felt part' of the activity.

Some students spoke passionately about their feelings of being ignored during lessons and the sense that this was unfair. For example, one girl explained how she would sometimes put her hand up to ask for advice. Seeing the teacher walking towards her, she would then be disappointed to see that an incident elsewhere in the classroom would then distract the teacher's attention. Other students argued that, despite the fact that they attended each day, working hard and always completing their homework on time, they rarely received commendations. Meanwhile they noticed that potentially disruptive students were often rewarded for what seemed like short periods of passive behaviour.

All the recordings were typed up fully so that the members of the staff inquiry team had access to what the students had said. This was felt to be crucial so that a sense of trust, authenticity and ownership was developed in the process. All names of teachers, students and obvious references to subjects were removed. This was not only to avoid finger-pointing and maintain the confidentiality of the students, but also to create a body of evidence of student experience that could apply to any individual and, therefore, potentially the responsibility of any staff member or indeed any student.

The observation notes and transcripts were then analysed and sections of dialogue on similar themes were grouped together. The team members identified any sections that jumped out at them – that made them stop and think, that taught them something new about their students and the practices and beliefs within the school. This process was repeated several times until, finally, the extracts were organised around the following themes: learning activities, copying, group work, getting help and having tasks explained, treatment of loud and quiet students, teacher talking, and praise for 'good' and 'bad' students.

Our observations of the discussions suggested that they led to the creation of a shared language, such that the team were able to communicate the subtleties of learning and teaching, diverse student needs, school ethos, and student voice. Naturally the conversations developed around what seemed to work and not work, as well as reflections about the teachers' own teaching and perceptions of learning. One of the teachers noted:

It became clear that these students were very aware that they got less attention or acknowledgement than other students and most of them felt that
this was unfair. They wanted to be recognised, not in an all-singing/danc-
ing fashion but to be given the opportunity to be recognised and acknowledged in ways that were appropriate to them. Some of them were very
aware that they were not known by certain staff even though they had
been in their lessons for over two years. They were also very clear about
the ways they liked to learn best and least.

She added:

They enjoyed lessons where they were actively involved in learning, where
they had to use their brains, where there was well-managed group work, or
where they felt they were part of the whole class learning together. They
disliked copying out of or taking notes from books, and they did not like
teachers who did not explain things clearly, check for understanding or
did not come round to give individual support. They were frustrated by
the fact that the pace of the lessons was dictated by the more outgoing or
challenging students.

Because the experience of gathering evidence had been powerful for the team
they decided to consult the head teacher about next steps. As a result, it was
decided that the findings should be presented at a meeting of the senior leadership team. At the meeting – which we attended – some senior colleagues were
evidently surprised and taken aback by the evidence. As a result, a whole school
meeting was arranged to discuss the implications of the evidence that had been
collected.

The meeting was held, after school, with over ninety members of staff and
several parent governors in attendance. The head introduced the event, then
some of the staff researchers explained the background to the project, how
they had gathered their evidence and their initial findings. All the staff were
then asked to discuss data extracts in small groups. From the amount of noise
and length of discussion it was reasonable to assume that the groups found the
data engaging. Comments overheard included: '. . . *amazing how powerful and clear
the student voice is*'; and '. . . *seems clear that there needs to be a review of teaching and learning styles to engage students' brains and recognise their presence as individuals*'.

Some scepticism was voiced about the validity of the data, based on the argument that it was only from a 'handful of students'. The response to this from
one member of the inquiry team was that the power of an individual dialogue
lies in how it clearly resonates with so many staff. This also led to a suggestion
from some staff that the process should be extended to other groups of students, and that it should also be repeated once some changes had been made
to see if and how they had impacted on the children. On leaving at the end of

the session, some teachers said they would go into their classrooms the following day and make an attempt to name and involve everyone. Whether this happened is not clear.

What was clear was the inquiry team's deepened understanding of the students' experiences and the role of the school processes in shaping these experiences. There was also a real sense of their becoming agents of change within the school, and equally powerful was their sense of the crucial different roles and skills that the different team members bring. As one of the team members commented, before this project she felt very much that her status was below that of other colleagues but now she realised she had an equally important role to play in exploring the student experience and bringing this to the attention of the whole staff.

Coming and going

Some schools addressed issues that are emerging as a challenge in many schools, particularly those in urban contexts. One of these issues is that of how to respond to new arrivals – both students transferring from other local schools and those arriving from elsewhere.

This became a burning issue at Highlands, a comprehensive school for 11- to 16-year-olds. When we got involved, the school had a student population of just over 400 students and served some of most disadvantaged communities in the country. The students were mainly British white, with a small number of Asian and African-Caribbean heritage students, and an increasing group of Eastern Europe white students for whom English was an additional language (EAL). At that time the school was undersubscribed and served a small housing estate with relatively low numbers of children of school age. Consequently, it had a very large number of feeder primary schools: twenty-four in all, with only 20 per cent of students living locally in a community that was also socio-economically disadvantaged. As a result, many students had long and sometimes difficult journeys to and from school.

The head teacher explained that, when he joined the school, it had what he described as a *'mentality of caring for its students'* but not one of improving life chances or attainment. Subsequently, the school had changed considerably, not least as result of a move into a new building. At the same time, it had changed its name and uniform. There were also substantial changes to its systems, practices and ethos.

Many of the staff were relatively new, including all the senior management team, with most having been there for no more than three or four years. A high proportion had middle management responsibilities and, because of the small size of the school, they often had to 'wear many hats'. As such, responsibilities sometimes seemed unclear and overlapping. It struck us that, within the inquiry team, this had helped to create a strong sense of joined-up responsibility, mutual respect for each other's contribution to the team's work regardless of position, openness and a clear shared goal of working to ensure the students have the best possible life chances.

The inquiry team members were: a deputy head with responsibility for inclusion, a head of one of the three houses, the special needs coordinator, a teaching assistant with responsibility for behaviour, and the inclusion administrator. The sixth team member was an advanced skills teacher (AST) in drama and the performing arts (ASTs are recognised as being highly skilled in relation to a particular subject and are expected to provide support for colleagues within their own schools and elsewhere). The head was keen to have a teacher with an arts specialism on the team since he was interested in how creativity might change people's lives *'by enabling people to be otherwise'*.

From the start, the team was keen to investigate issues around mobility in terms of the significantly high number of students who were arriving after the start of Year 7, some of whom moved to Highlands to avoid permanent exclusion from previous schools. The team was also concerned about the number of students for whom Highlands was their second choice. Apparently, the pattern was that some of these chose to leave when places eventually came up in their first-choice school.

The team felt that many parents had relatively negative images of the school, largely based on its past reputation. They were also aware that there was no robust induction process in the school for new arrivals and that it was often difficult to get data about students from their previous schools. They suspected, too, that some of these new students felt isolated, both with respect to their classmates and the teachers. An added challenge to all of this came as a result of a sudden intake of EAL students that, we were told, had 'caught the school on the hop'. Some indications of racism had surfaced as a consequence of this intake and, as a result, staff had attempted to develop processes to support the full participation of these students in school life.

A group of eight students who had arrived at the school in Year 10 and 11 were selected. The staff team decided to compare the experiences of these students with those of another group who had been in the school since the start of Year 7. This group comprised five girls and one boy, all said to be of relatively high ability. One of the team devised a questionnaire comprising mainly open questions about subject choices, awareness of expected exam grades, confidence in achieving grades, preferred subjects, career choices and aspirations, making friends, and belonging to Highlands. The questionnaires were then used as the basis of focus group discussions and the students also completed them individually. The 'mobile students' were divided into two groups of four, as it was felt this would give them more space to speak. This was also to avoid potential disruptive behaviour from two of the students if put together. The students who had been in the school longer discussed the issues as one group.

One of the university team facilitated the focus groups so that the students would feel more able to express themselves. The head of house and the teaching assistant were also present. They commented later that their presence did not appear to impact on the established group but sensed it might have done with the mobile groups, since the students had not built up a sense of trust with the staff of how honest they could be.

The staff team then scrutinised the transcripts – in a way similar to teachers at Valley High – in order to identify sections of dialogue that stood out, and collated the responses to the questionnaire. They were clearly taken aback by the findings. Significant to them was the difference between the general sense of well-being of the established group and the discomfort that many of the mobile students were experiencing. They had also expected social issues to be the mobile students' main concern but this did not turn out to be the case.

The established students generally felt supported by the school – there was a sense that they had been given a lot of help and advice by staff. They had all been able to take their first choices in their subjects; they were mainly clear what their expected grades were; they felt they could approach members of staff; and they felt they were known and knew everyone, and that they belonged to the school. In contrast, the mobile group felt a lot less confident about their subjects. Surprisingly, for the staff, this seemed more important to them than the social side of their settling-in process. They were not clear what their expected grades were, most of them had not been able to take their first choices in subjects, they were not fully aware of the range of choices they had, and some of them felt they had been placed in classes in an ad hoc fashion. As regards course work, many of these students felt frustrated that work for exam subjects from their previous schools was not acknowledged. In some cases, too, they felt they were viewed negatively for not having done the appropriate course work and, consequently, not given any support to catch up. The group also talked about not feeling as if they belonged and the difficulty of building up a sense of being known, as well as knowing what to expect from staff and students. They talked poignantly about the benefits of going to school with the children who you grow up with 'on your street'. In addition, some of them commented on how friendly and willing to help they had found many of the staff, and some speculated this was probably because of the school's relatively small size.

The inquiry team decided to observe newly arrived students in class to see what their experiences of learning and interactions appeared to be. Ideally they would have liked to observe the same Year 11 students they had talked to in the previous discussions. However, it was felt this might be too distracting at an important time of year for these students. Also, the students might be aware of the purpose and react to the presence of the inquiry team member. Instead, five Year 9 students who had arrived in the previous month were identified.

The evidence generated showed that the newly-arrived students interacted in similar ways. Most of them seemed – in varying degrees – to be awkward and self-conscious, and in some cases lacking in confidence. In general they seemed to be relatively eager to please both the teacher and their peers. Ongoing negotiation of friendships was evident, sometimes resulting in their being drawn quietly into off-task activities.

The students responded well to attention from the teachers, although on one occasion they were completely ignored. When given attention, they evidently grew in confidence as the lessons proceeded. Attention involved directing easily answerable questions at the new students, providing extra attention on a one-to-one basis, working through examples with them and naming them more than other students.

Looked at alongside the views of students, the evidence gathered by observation provided a stimulus for discussing the experiences of these young people and, as a consequence, ways of responding. At another level, this began the process of creating a shared language – in a similar way to the staff at Valley High – where the team was able to communicate the subtleties of school processes in relation to student differences. Naturally the conversations developed around potential strategies, as well as reflections about the team's own practices and beliefs about teaching, learning and schooling. One member explained:

> We were taken aback by how the school transition experience had impacted on the mobile students, especially in terms of how they viewed their academic experiences rather than, as many of us had assumed, their social situations. This was regardless of the students' behaviour or ability. As a result of our investigations, we made changes to our admissions process, refined the options process and made sure that each new student was assigned a key worker to support their integration into Highlands.

The team acted quickly on their engagement with the evidence. The admissions process was reviewed and new students were met in person by their head of house in order to complete their options process. In addition, the option process was refined. It was agreed that new arrivals would start on a Friday, to meet their tutor and be assigned a 'buddy', before beginning school formally on the following Monday. The inclusion administrator would act as the key worker for all new arrivals.

Overall, what emerged during that year was a deepening understanding of the students' experiences and the role of the school processes in shaping these experiences. The following year saw an increasing number of new arrivals to Highlands, including many more for whom English was an additional language

(EAL). Focusing attention on this particular group of students seemed a natural progression. The inquiry team all felt that these students were not receiving an equitable education and wanted to investigate their hunch further. Explaining the situation, a member of staff said:

> Although our total school population fluctuates, as does our EAL population, approximately 8 per cent of our students now have EAL – therefore a hugely significant cohort. Interestingly, there are an additional eleven first languages spoken by our students, in addition to English, with Slovakian, Punjabi and Polish being the most spoken.

The team decided to address the following questions: to what extent are the EAL students engaged in learning in the classroom, and how do staff members include them in learning? How do our EAL students feel about their school experiences and do they feel that they are equally valued as members of the school community? And, what systems can we use that will clearly assess these students in order to ensure their learning needs are fully met?

One of the teachers outlined what they did:

> Last year the use of lesson observations proved to be very informative. We used an observation schedule designed with the help of the university. It focused on the classroom interactions of the students in relation to their interactions with teachers, their tasks and their peers. We carried out similar observations of our EAL students. These were followed up by recorded interviews with the students, carried out by the researchers and witnessed by one of our equity team members.

The evidence generated through the student observations showed that the EAL students interacted in similar ways. As in the previous year, to varying degrees they all seemed to be awkward and self-conscious, and in many cases lacking in confidence. What was apparent was that they generally seemed to be relatively eager to please both the teacher and their peers. It was apparent in a number of observations that the very new arrivals seemed to rely heavily on the support of other EAL students who had been in the school longer. It was felt that these 'older' students may well have their progress hindered by helping others to progress rather than focusing on themselves. In all cases, as the team had anticipated, it was apparent that learning was hindered by the barrier of an unfamiliar language.

During the focus group discussions there was further evidence that the students themselves felt this and, indeed, wanted extra tuition in English. One colleague commented that some of the students also seemed to struggle with literacy. An immediate concern that came out of these interviews was the fact that all the EAL students had experiences of bullying, either first-hand or as witnesses. As a result, they were afraid of being labelled as 'different', had

suffered loss of confidence and, for some, had low self-esteem. On a more positive note, what was pleasing was their very positive attitude towards school. It was
evident that this was a set of students who really wanted to learn and were willing
to work hard to make progress. The one thing that every student mentioned was
the excellent facilities in the school, especially in terms of ICT equipment.

Additional evidence already existed in the school in the form of attitude- and
behaviour-tracking data systems. Our experience is that many schools are rich
in such data but it is often not used effectively for strategic purposes. The team
wanted to see how they could draw on this information to gain further insight
into the experiences of the EAL students.

The chart in Figure 4.1 was based on the first sixteen weeks at Highlands of
the EAL students who formed the focus group. It gives an indication of how
each student settled in the school and provides information about their participation and achievements, and whether these were recognised by staff. So, for
example, the staff team noted that Alicia, in particular, seemed to have 'settled
down quickly' and was frequently rewarded, whereas Esme and Catarina could
have benefited from additional support to encourage further participation.

The two charts in Figure 4.2 show the types of positive behaviour recorded
for each student and give a more detailed picture of how the students were
participating. What stood out for the staff was how Ali's experience seemed
to be much more positive than Esme's, as demonstrated by the variety of
behaviours shown, covering many different areas such as teamwork, helping

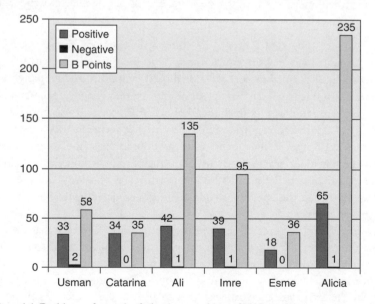

Figure 4.1 Positive and negative behaviour tracking of EAL students

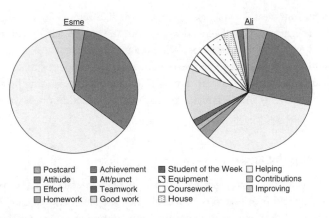

☐ Postcard	■ Achievement	■ Student of the Week	☐ Helping
■ Attitude	■ Att/punct	◨ Equipment	☐ Contributions
☐ Effort	■ Teamwork	☐ Coursework	☐ Improving
■ Homework	☐ Good work	▦ House	

Figure 4.2 Student profiles of behaviour and participation

others, making contributions to the House and so on. Esme's behaviour, on the other hand, appeared to be more restricted, focusing on attitude, effort and good work (acknowledged through a postcard sent home), suggesting a more limited participation.

Using this available data early on in a new student's life proved to be helpful in tracking how well a student was settling in and, in this way, served as an early warning sign in identifying needs and concerns, allowing for intervention to take place.

Using the tracking data also provided additional information about how EAL students felt about themselves and their learning experience. These data were also compared with a group of non-EAL students. The graph in Figure 4.3, which

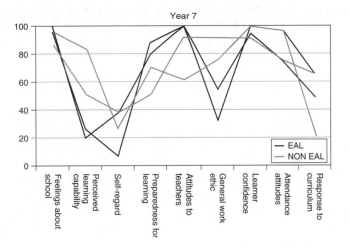

Figure 4.3 Comparison of EAL and non-EAL students' attitudes to self and school

focuses on four Year 7 students, suggests a huge difference in self-regard, perceived learning capacity and general work ethic. In fact, the self-regard factor was strikingly low in all the year groups – clearly an area requiring attention.

A number of further changes were made as a direct result of this stage of the investigation. In particular, staff development activities regarding how to integrate EAL students into lessons were introduced. In addition, a weekly EAL support group was set up.

Rethinking the agenda

In some instances an engagement with evidence led staff to have to rethink the way they had formulated their initial agendas. This happened at Westbury High, a school that had approximately 40 per cent Asian heritage and 60 per cent white British students. There was also an increasing number of refugee and asylum seekers from a wide variety of countries. The Asian British students mainly came from a district that experienced multiple deprivations.

A decade or so earlier, the comprehensive schools in the centre of the town had poor reputations and many families turned to the two selective grammar schools. If they did not get into one of these, the next choice was usually Westbury. This established a pattern that has continued, even though Central High, nearby, had improved significantly. Another reason why this pattern had been sustained could have been because some parents preferred to send their children to a more culturally mixed school, since Central High was predominantly Asian heritage.

The community surrounding Westbury comprises almost 100 per cent white British who are traditionally working class. Some families chose not to send their children to Westbury because of its ethnic mix. Within the school, the students from different ethnic backgrounds were generally harmonious and worked well together. Within classrooms strict seating plans were used to mix students by ethnicity and gender.

In joining SERN, the head teacher and her senior colleagues decided that they wanted to investigate disaffection in the school. Seven boys had been permanently excluded during the previous year and it had been noted that a disproportionate number of these students, five in all, had been of Asian heritage. The senior staff assumed these difficulties were related to the boys being part of a youth subculture within the Asian community, and a problematic generation gap between the boys and their parents. Their initial focus was to try and reduce the amount of permanent exclusions amongst some of their disaffected Asian British males. In 2006-7 they had seven permanent exclusions, five of which were for young Asian British males. The exclusions were related to violence or drugs. One of their senior staff explained:

On the whole [the exclusions] were not for one-off incidents but rather for series of incidents that we could not find a way through to resolving successfully . . . . Our approach first and foremost is to support the student, and permanent exclusion is very much a last resort for us.

He went on to explain that when issues arose with these boys, they generally had parental support for how they dealt with them, adding:

it was very rare that a parent wasn't working alongside us to try and find a successful solution.

However, in these cases, they were not able to find a way of addressing these students' needs.

The senior teacher added that the boys had shown signs of disaffection lower down the school. When asked if the staff had felt this might be related to ethnicity or culture, he talked about his belief that these young people's parents were probably relatively unaware of their children's lifestyles outside of the family home. Based on glimpses of a subculture, which some members of staff had gleaned from hearing informal conversations between students, they also suspected that these students came into contact with drug-related activities, organised fights and a gang culture. Regarding the comment about students' views on the seriousness of exclusion, the one thing they all had in common was that they did think it was serious.

The staff inquiry team, led by a deputy head, identified twenty-six students whose behaviour had given most concern. These included both Asian and white British students – twenty-four of them turned out to be boys and most were from Years 8 to 10. A behaviour database was used to carry out this analysis, although later members of the team realised they could have gone on hunches.

The staff conducted focus group discussions for each year group, all of which were prompted by similar questions, facilitated by researchers from the university, and observed by a member of the pastoral team. In addition, some staff were interviewed about their views about exclusions and students' behaviour.

In general the students recognised that they displayed challenging behaviour in school. They felt that, whilst they were often punished because of this, the school's actions were generally fair. They did not pick out any particular teachers or subjects where they felt they were treated less fairly than other students, or where they behaved more badly. They tended to share similar views about lessons, learning, being punished and reasons for feeling disaffected regardless of their ethnicity, and none of their reasons for challenging behaviour and disaffection appeared to be related to race issues. All the students realised that exclusion was serious and that it significantly impacted on future career opportunities. They also commented that their parents would be upset and disappointed in them if they were excluded.

The focus of attention changed, however, when, on closer analysis it became evident that a common feature of all of these students – white and Asian heritage – was that they all had reading levels significantly lower than their chronological reading ages, in some cases by more than three years. In contrast, only one out of them recognised that he had a reading problem, and that was a Year 7 student. Clearly this could be because the students did not want to see themselves as having a weakness, or because they saw 'getting by' as being enough.

The deputy head explained that they had found about 40 per cent of all their students between Years 7 to 11 had reading levels below their chronological reading ages, with some of the gaps being '*absolutely shocking*'. He added that staff were not fully aware of this figure and, similarly, they were probably not fully aware of those young people in their lessons who had weak reading and writing skills, nor the extent of their struggle. Despite some of them knowing about the low levels of literacy across the school, it was still, he explained, 'confronting' to see the correlation between low reading ages and disaffection for the focus groups. Although a relatively small number of the students might have been excluded due to serious disaffection, this statistic might have indicated a much larger number of students who were not as engaged as they could be because of literacy.

The teacher gave an example of another teacher, not knowing a student very well, who asked them to read in front of a class. Rather than admit to their inability to read, the student might respond with challenging behaviour or, less evidently, simply switch off. He added that learning outcomes tended to dip towards the end of Year 7 and during Year 8, not just because of impending adolescence and peer pressure, but also because students found reading and writing a lot harder, '*and there is suddenly a lot more of it at a higher level*'.

As a result of this rethinking, in the following school year attention was focused on ways of fostering literacy across the curriculum, particularly in Years 7 and 8.

Alternative explanations

We saw a similar process of rethinking brought about as a result of an engagement with evidence at Southdale High. This led the staff inquiry group there to consider a range of explanations before deciding what actions to take.

Southdale set out to provide a wide range of high-quality sporting, dance and drama opportunities for its students. It also strove to be inclusive and equitable for all of its students. Many students benefited from this provision, with a significant number competing and performing at relatively high-stake events. However, the staff inquiry team were concerned that there was a persistent group who were only partly engaged, and did not seem to benefit from the school as much as they could. This was most evident in these students' lack of participation in out-of-school-hours (OOSH) activities, especially sports, dance and theatre.

The team started from an assumption that extracurricular activities have a positive impact on learning and achievement, and on the attitude of students who choose to participate. In relation to this assumption, they also had a hunch that the students who participated least were, in the staff's terms, middle to lower ability girls, coming mainly from an area of social disadvantage. With all of this in mind, they set out to find out who exactly the students were who participated or did not participate in OOSH activities, their views about school and these activities, their characteristics and their levels of progress.

The head teacher asked one of the deputy heads to lead the work, although, as will become clear, later he felt the members of the team drove the project together. The team members were selected on the basis of their varied ideas and viewpoints, and their capacity to lead the project. They were: a PE teacher who ran a lot of extracurricular activities and was also the transition coordinator between Years 6 and 7; the head of Year 7, who was interested in how the students got involved in school as they settled in; a teaching assistant who worked with some of the most disaffected students, and so was interested in students who were perhaps not excluded but found participation in school life and learning challenging; and a teacher who was studying for a Master's degree in education, and so was interested in the concept of using research in school and exploring aspects of education that went beyond her immediate role as a teacher. The deputy head, who was in charge of pastoral care and, therefore, felt he was particularly student-focused, also had a leading role in the use of statistical data across the school.

The team met regularly every three to four weeks before school for about 45 minutes. One teacher explained:

> We feel it has been very important to establish this pattern early on. Our approach was also beneficial. We were quite pragmatic and task driven, setting ourselves deadlines to complete activities by, for example, we set aside one meeting to create our questionnaire; another to collate our findings, and another to discuss them; we did not reflect and discuss continuously but gave ourselves clear space to do this once we had enough data in. It was not led by the deputy head telling everyone what to do – rather people volunteered to do certain things depending on their availability and skills. The deputy organised the meetings and cover arrangements where necessary. We also swopped roles frequently to keep the dynamic going. There was a sense that we were all in this together.

In thinking about their investigations they were aware that, nationally, there was a lot of evidence about 'drop-off' in Year 8, when students start to be less engaged in school activities and where academic standards start to slip. They therefore decided to look at students in terms of their participation in OOSH activities but also their more general participation and sense of involvement in school. To do this they had to look at students who had already been through this phase, so they focused on Year 9, a group of 243 students.

The first stage of their research was to gather information from the Year 9 students about their participation in OOSH activities. To do this, they devised a questionnaire that asked students to identify themselves, as follows:

Group A – those who participate in extracurricular activities;
Group B – those who had taken part in the past but who no longer take part in
           any activities; or
Group C – those who had never taken part in any activity.

The students were also asked to give additional details, such as how many activities they took part or had taken part in, when and why they stopped taking part, or why they had never been involved.

The pie chart (Figure 4.4) shows the breakdown of students in each of the groups. Reflecting on this, the deputy head commented:

> We were encouraged by the number of students who continued to do extracurricular activities, and we were not surprised by the number of students who had never taken part in activities since we knew that this was a consequence of them having to travel long distances to school or because they were involved in activities out of school such as theatre, dance groups or horse riding, for example. However, we were concerned about the slightly larger-than-expected number of students who had once attended OOSH activities but no longer did, and by the fact that the drop-out point was significant in Year 8. There was no noticeable difference between the figures for boys and girls.

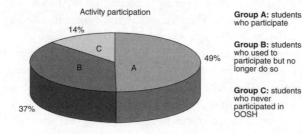

Figure 4.4 Participation of Year 9 students in OOSH activities

The additional details were used to identify students for the next stage of the research. From a total of 89 out of 243 students in Group B, the inquiry team identified 23 to take part in focus group discussions.

Each of the Group B discussions consisted of between five and eight students and was facilitated by university researchers, with a member of the staff inquiry team present; Group A focus groups were facilitated by Southdale staff, who had observed the Group B focus groups. The students were encouraged to discuss why they had stopped doing extracurricular activities and why they believed other students continue to do these activities. In addition, they were asked about what the students thought about their school; and what activities they liked doing where they felt they were learning and involved and the converse of these. They were also asked if they felt cared for, safe and whether they were treated fairly. The aim of asking these questions was to see if they surfaced other experiences or processes at work in the school that might provide leads to why students dropped out of OOSH activities.

In general, students from Group B spoke positively about their experiences of school; for example, they said that the school was 'like a family', mainly because all their friends were there. Regarding their learning experiences, they were mostly positive, especially about certain ways of learning. They all liked lessons that were practical, active or, in the case of writing, they liked using it to record an activity conducted earlier, or in a way that was relevant to everyday life such as writing a persuasive letter. They liked learning where everyone in the class was involved, and where it required them to create something that seemed relevant. Having choice over subjects to study was also important to them and how they applied themselves.

However, these students also made comments that started to raise other issues regarding their experiences. Many said that when they started at the school, the first thing that struck them was the size of the school. Reference was made to the need to 'try and fit in', otherwise they might get 'picked on'. This sentiment of wanting to 'fit in' – which we interpreted as a kind of peer pressure in relation to a sense of self-worth – seemed to be echoed elsewhere when these students explained why they did not continue doing OOSH activities. Reasons given included the belief that you had 'to be good' to do them. Another was the fear of being laughed at by the 'noisier', 'more popular', 'more confident' students if they did something wrong or not very well.

Some of these students felt they needed their friends to go with them to OOSH activities, as other students seemed confident and in cliques, and they felt too nervous on their own. Bullying was identified as an issue for some students, and although systems were in place to deal with it, and they felt comfortable about telling a member of staff, bullying was still going on.

The fear of peers' opinions was echoed when some of the students talked about activities that required some form of public performance or public assessment. One student disliked sharing his writing with other students because he was 'rubbish' at it, and felt he would get laughed at. Another was worried about being called 'a swot'.

When talking more generally about experiences of the curriculum, some of these students believed noisier or more confident students got more attention from teachers than they did. Some wanted more help and support but did not know how to get attention in ways that were not quickly overshadowed by more confident students, who would somehow divert teachers' attention. These students perceived students from Group A (i.e. those who continue to do OOSH activities) as being already confident but that this was helped through doing OOSH activities.

Students in Group A, by contrast, felt they were not influenced by their peers when becoming involved in OOSH activities. They were involved because they really wanted to be – they were choosing for themselves to do something they enjoyed. They were also aware of the benefits of participating in extracurricular activities; for example, some even said it might help their grades. Others said they liked the related curriculum lessons and it sometimes helped to improve their relationships with staff. Overall, these students appeared much more self-confident and independent. They were also aware of the responsibility of committing to doing an OOSH activity, and some of them expressed a sense of pride at this commitment.

The staff team wanted to see if there was any correlation between the patterns of participation in OOSH activities, the academic progress of students, and where they lived. The next step was therefore to look at academic progress. With this in mind, they looked at Cognitive Abilities Tests (CATs) scores when students first came to the school, and assessment of core subjects given by teachers throughout their time at Southdale. They also looked at the students' postcodes to see if any patterns emerged in relation to housing and neighbourhoods.

They found no patterns between where students lived and participation. Regarding academic progress, the Group A and B students all started the school in Year 7 with similar CATs scores, although Group A students had subsequently made better progress in terms of English, Maths and Science (Figure 4.5).

In short, the staff team realised that there *was* a link between participation in OOSH activities and academic progress rates. However, rather than being a causal relationship, this appeared to be more complex. Although there appeared to be little difference in the areas where the students in Group A and B came from, nor in their academic levels when they first arrived at the school, they appeared to have significant differences in their confidence levels and their

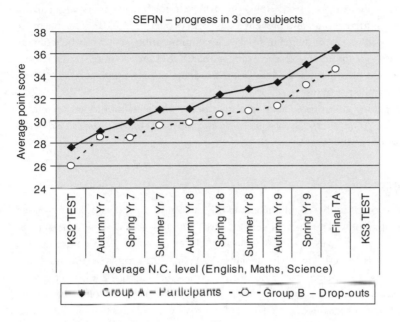

Figure 4.5 Groups A and B progress from Year 7 to the end of Year 9

sense of self-worth, both in terms of OOSH activities and across the curriculum. They also seemed to believe that some students got treated differently, or were able to garner a different kind of attention, depending on their confidence and their abilities. In other words, participation in OOSH activities seemed to be associated with the way they were dealt with in the school and this, in turn, appeared to have an impact on their views of themselves as learners and on their academic progress.

Whilst the inquiry team's initial hunch focused on provision and the belief that if students participate in OOSH activities they were more likely to have a more positive experience in school, these findings shifted their focus to the individual student: first, in terms of building confidence, self-esteem and raising aspirations through personal relationships, both in the classroom and in OOSH activities; and, second, in raising staff awareness of individual needs and how to respond to them.

In the light of their investigations, the staff team decided to take the following actions: raise awareness in the school by sharing the findings across the whole school and asking staff to become involved in discussing the implications; look at using sixth form mentors to support individuals and groups in schools by helping to raise their confidence, their attendance and their attitudes to school; examine the school's social and emotional aspects of its learning programme with a view to helping promote self-confidence; work with current Year 7 students to try and prevent a dip from occurring in Year 8; enable more students to perform drama in smaller, less intimidating, groups and encourage parents to come and watch and examine the OOSH provision to see if anything else could be done to encourage more students to participate and, as a result, improve their progress in school.

In talking about these actions, a member of the staff inquiry group added: *'If we can get five teachers to notice fifteen students they might not otherwise notice then that should have a major impact'.*

Conclusion

The accounts in this chapter illustrate how a common process of inquiry-based development was interpreted very differently in each school. At a general level, the accounts suggest a similar pattern of development in each context as the staff teams moved from their initial focus on particular groups of students – presumed to be vulnerable to various forms of marginalisation – towards a focus on contextual factors that created barriers for these groups. In so doing, this moved attention to processes of overall school improvement in ways that had the potential to improve conditions for larger numbers of learners within a school.

In all four schools, marked shifts became evident at both the individual and team levels, as evidence contradicted and elaborated prior understandings. It was significant that the extent to which a relatively narrow initial focus widened as a result of the process was shaped significantly by the willingness of school leaders to allow these issues to be explored and by the wider culture of the school. Each team found ways of developing its practice in response to the process. However, external policy constraints opened some channels of development whilst closing many others.

In some schools, as we saw, the teams went on to share their evidence with their colleagues at department or whole school meetings. These, to varying degrees, challenged and stimulated some staff's thinking, and in some instances they caused a degree of discomfort. The teams sometimes encountered opposition from colleagues who refused to accept the meaning of the evidence they had generated. In such contexts, evidence generated from student 'voice' proved to be particularly powerful in challenging established meanings.

Some of the investigations led on to changes and developments in practices in the schools. These ranged from embedding mutual observations amongst groups of staff, to making procedural changes to admissions of new students starting outside the normal starting time, to more subtle individual changes relating to how the staff interacted with students in class and organised group activities.

The accounts are, in many senses, very encouraging. They demonstrate the potential of groups of schools to work together, using various kinds of evidence to challenge inequities within their organisational contexts. At the same time, local historical factors continued to limit the impact of their efforts. In particular, trends within the 'market place' of the local education system made some of the partner schools extremely vulnerable. This is a key issue that we return to in later chapters. Meanwhile, in the next chapter we look in more detail at what is involved in using evidence in strategic ways to foster equitable school development. In so doing, we also elaborate on some of the difficulties we have had to address in using this approach within the SERN schools.

5 Making sense of the process

Previous chapters have outlined the development of SERN and described in some detail the projects developed within four of the schools. In this chapter we begin to analyse what we saw taking place in the schools, once again using examples, in order to draw out common features and problems associated with bringing about changes in practice. These examples remind us that changing practice – even when the change is quite modest – is a complex process. They also reveal some of the barriers encountered *within* schools by team members attempting to take a lead in the change process. At the same time they illustrate how inquiry can be used as a catalyst for change.

In compiling these accounts we are reminded that, despite the close working relationships we fostered with certain members of staff within the network schools, we remained outsiders, with only partial understandings of what was happening on a day-to-day basis within these school communities. Acknowledging this limitation, in what follows we reflect on what we saw happening over the five years, as project teams in the schools attempted to implement the ideas and approaches we had developed with them. As anticipated, in each case implementation involved important processes of adaptation, as those involved interpreted and made their own sense of these ideas, to fit their own schools and particular circumstances. As we will seek to illustrate, these actions also took place in contexts where there were other factors at work, influencing and to some extent even shaping developments.

In scrutinising these processes we make use of an adapted version of a typology developed by House (1979) to model what happens during educational innovation, which he defines as *'the deliberate systematic attempt to change the school through introducing new ideas and techniques'* (p. 137). This typology proposes three ways of thinking about the implementation process:

1. *A technical view*, which treats innovation as a systematic, rational-technical process made up of separate functions and components.

2. *A political view*, which draws attention to how innovations impact on existing power relationships, often leading to struggles between individuals or groups who adopt positions that defend their interests.
3. *A cultural view*, which focuses on the ways that existing roles, attitudes and beliefs within a given social setting are disturbed by change, which may lead to resistance.

We use these perspectives as lenses through which developments within the schools during the project can be viewed. In this way we seek to demonstrate both the richness and complexity of the change process, and the multiple realities that complicate the way practitioners think about their own practice.

School change as a series of technical processes

Given the very different school contexts, it was hardly surprising that the ways the school teams conceptualised their roles and went about their task varied considerably. Adopting a technical perspective, we examine some of the ways the teams approached their tasks. This enables us to identify separate stages within the overall processes that were common across the schools, though different in detail. Typically, these started with a move from initial hunches to specific questions, informed through engagement with data already available, followed by a data gathering exercise, which extended to include evidence from and in many cases collected by students, and finally analysis and actions.

Starting with hunches

As we have explained, the starting point each year for the work of the schools involved in SERN was an initial workshop, where the inquiry teams identified and refined their areas of focus for the coming year. Reflecting on provision in their schools to identify groups of students they suspected might be in some way missing out, they were encouraged initially to articulate their hunches about groups of students that might, for whatever reason, be less well served than others.

Exploring their hunches further, the school teams were encouraged to speculate about possible reasons for these perceived inequities. Sometimes, they confessed that they simply did not know the reasons, but nevertheless had 'worries' about particular groups. In other cases difficulties were explained in terms of what we might describe as problems associated with particular students – essentially a learner-deficit approach. For example, different teams talked about groups of students who were perhaps being marginalised because they were: middle-to-low ability and mildly disaffected; unable to keep up because

English was for them an additional language; regularly missing from school; unrealistically high in their aspirations for their ability level; more concerned with making friends and establishing their social standing; new to the school after the normal starting date; or repeatedly in detention because they refused to comply with the school behaviour strategy.

Once staff had articulated their hunches, they went through the process of narrowing these down to a specific target group for investigation, and began to plan how they would carry out their investigations. This often proved to be a lengthy process, one that varied across the schools. Back in their schools, the teams then set about finding out more about the identified student group, gaining a clearer picture of their characteristics and experiences. As we saw in the previous chapter, this process sometimes led to surprises, as the teams found that their assumptions about the experiences and attitudes of these students, and their vulnerabilities, were not as they had expected.

Reviewing existing data

Often the teams used existing statistical data as the starting point for their inquiries, scanning this for general patterns or differences. All of the schools, it seemed, routinely gathered more data about students than they had found time to analyse. Even at this early stage in the investigations, in some instances these data challenged initial assumptions. Going back to Valley High, for example, we saw how the staff team used data derived from the school's behaviour management system to identify students who did not seem to attract attention, be it positive or negative, whom they referred to as 'invisible children'. At Long Road – where the staff team was much engaged by Valley's inquiry into the experiences of these children – the hunch was that they too had a group of overlooked students. Here, they called them their 'wallpaper children'. Further, the expectation within the team was that when they had identified this group, they could predict a number of characteristics they would share.

They speculated, in particular, that the students came from the same areas, so they looked at which primary schools students had attended and their home address postcodes. They also speculated that dates of birth would reveal a pattern, thinking that there might be a significant number of younger children from the year in this group. At the same time, they predicted that the attendance levels of these students would be poor. Armed with these initial ideas, they began to look at the student data within their own behaviour management system, and sure enough identified a group that seemed not to appear very often – again attracting neither negative nor positive attention.

In fact, they discovered there were no obvious patterns to be found in these data that confirmed any of these speculations. This led one teacher to comment, '*The danger is when you think there is a common thread you start trying to find something that isn't there*'. She went on to describe how staff can easily create stories around students from small pieces of information that stereotype them, then develop policies to deal with the stereotype. The problem is that in reality there are not groups of students who match these stereotypes.

Looking again at these students, the team members were struck by how easily they had been drawn to negative assumptions about them. In fact, the students they had identified shared few characteristics, and for the most part were not underachieving – 80 per cent of them were at or above learning targets. This demonstrated that the teachers' knowledge of their students could be influenced by perceptions that were rooted in their own thinking patterns, rather than the actual behaviour of the students. One teacher reflected on what she had discovered about the 'wallpaper' children, '*They were literate and articulate . . . they weren't actually without the power of expression*'.

These discoveries prompted the staff team towards direct engagement with the students in order to find out more. Specifically, the team decided they would focus on all students currently in Year 8, and gather from them views about their experiences, good and bad, within the school. They decided to do this using a survey instrument, one they would develop in cooperation with the students.

In other schools, too, the engagement with existing data sometimes led to confusion and dead-ends. We have already described how the staff team at Moorside High knew that their school had a problem with attendance. Indeed, at the time the school had one of the poorest attendance records in the country. During their initial discussions the team speculated about possible causes; for example, parental and community attitudes, teacher attitudes, and home difficulties. They decided they would also investigate feeder primary school statistics. In the end, they had defined over a dozen ways to identify a group to focus on and commented that they felt overwhelmed. Many of these ways proved difficult to organise, requiring data-gathering from diverse groups often outside of the school. Even so, they were reluctant to give up any of their identified sources.

Generating questions

Having identified a focus for their inquiries through a consideration of existing data, the teams generally felt they needed to collect additional evidence in order to better understand what it meant to be within those groups of learners. This led them to consider what sorts of questions would generate the data they needed, and how and from whom these data could be collected.

In general – as we saw in the previous chapter – as teachers engaged in this process they moved on from seeking explanations rooted in the characteristics of the students themselves, towards an exploration of contextual factors – such as the curriculum, teaching practices, attitudes, relationships and even pre-entry and post-school pathways – that might bear on the experiences and attitudes of these learners. In many cases the process also moved them towards an increased desire to involve the students themselves and other less obvious participants in the data gathering and analysis processes.

The need for data brought with it the need to identify how and where this would be generated. In the main, this would involve the use of various forms of observation and group interview techniques. Such approaches were deliberately used in an eclectic way so that different teams could address the specific parameters, constraints and objectives of their particular project.

As outsiders we noted that unexpected insights often emerged from discussions within the teams about where the focus for the project should lie and what questions needed to be asked in order to fully understand the experiences of the particular student groups identified for attention. Such insights sometimes led to shifts in their understandings of ways inequities were perceived and experienced by their students. Together, these shifts revealed strong indications of how collective engagement with evidence can help staff in school to rethink their assumptions about the nature and impact of marginalisation.

Gathering additional data

In several of the schools, the teams opted for observation schedules that sought to see lessons through the students' eyes. Consequently, many of these schedules focused on the teacher's performance rather than the students. Typically, different staff members observed students in different lessons and then shared the written summaries they had produced. The names of teachers, students and subjects were removed, with the aim of avoiding conversations around performance or individuals. This process enabled staff groups to discuss broader issues, such as teaching methods, observable evidence of learning, teacher-student interactions and relationships, and student interactions with peers during lessons. How staff reacted to the data varied between schools.

Staff at Valley High were taken aback by how similar the observed student interactions and experiences appeared to be. Their discussions gradually became more reflective, with staff talking more generally about students' experiences and contextual factors within the school that might bear on the student interactions. By contrast, the original project team at Central High seemed less surprised by the experiences of their students. They noted that many appeared uninspired and even disengaged, showing little commitment to complete tasks. Some students also appeared to have problems understanding instructions or concepts central to the lesson, resorting to copying answers from the board or peers, and chatting. There seemed to be some reluctance amongst the staff to broaden the conversation out to discuss what was happening around the students that might explain these behaviours.

At Southside, the team felt that – for ethical reasons – it was important to tell the teachers in advance which students were being observed in their lessons. Arguably, this affected how the teacher then interacted with these students, often resulting in them receiving more attention than they might otherwise have done. However, it could be argued that this in itself may lead to fruitful discussions about things that happen in classrooms which teachers are loathe to display to their colleagues.

As we have reported, other forms of observation data were generated. For example, some of the schools invited pairs of students to take photographs around the school of places where they felt comfortable or uncomfortable. These were then used to create collage-type posters on which the students summarised their views, and which became the basis for discussions among teachers.

In trying to establish how students felt about core and foundation subjects, the equity team at Leafy Top High organised 'learning walks'. These involved students taking members of the team round the school, by whichever route they preferred, and talking staff through experiences they had in each of the areas and how they felt about them. In addition to finding out how students felt about different subjects, the staff were surprised by the incidental matters that cropped up while doing these student-led walks. For example, some students commented that they '*never normally get picked for things*', and others talked about how they felt in the corridors between lessons. Staff commented on the value of '*just spending time with the students*', sharing their experiences of what being in the school felt like.

However, some of the teams found it difficult to make sense of their observations, other than through the lens of individual teacher performance. Indeed, we were surprised by how keen teachers were to feed back the students' experiences during lessons to their teachers. A concern was this could potentially undermine the trust between colleagues – something that in our experience is essential for meaningful scrutiny of current practices – and thus reduce the impact of the project. However, perhaps such inclinations are the product of a policy context where classroom observation is usually associated with teacher appraisal and performance management procedures.

The team at Valley High discussed the idea that perhaps the overlooked students they were observing did not want to be 'picked on' or 'exposed' in front of their peers. This led to a discussion about how they could discover what the students felt without embarrassing them, and the use of student focus groups. The team in another school, Long Road, was surprised to find that contrary to their expectations, their invisible students all wanted to feel acknowledged in lessons, although exactly how might be different for different students. These students were also aware that other students – both 'naughty' and more confident students – got more attention than they did.

In several of the schools the teams choose at some point to conduct focus groups with students. Typically, these would comprise four to six students and a facilitator. In most cases a member of the university team took on this role, on the assumption that students would express their views more openly with an outsider. Interestingly, teachers in one school felt strongly that this had the opposite effect, since in talking to outsiders the students would want to be loyal to their school.

In order to build their own capacity to conduct such interviews and ensure transparency, staff sometimes sat in during these discussions. Whether or not to include a member of staff in the focus group facilitation or recording process often presented a dilemma between, on the one hand, enabling the students to speak freely and, on the other hand, including staff in the process. Meanwhile, the Moorside team preferred to develop their own focus group exercise. Described as 'workshops', these involved what seemed to us to be somewhat chaotic activities with between ten and fifteen students. Nevertheless, it was evident that interesting material was generated from this activity and the process had the advantage that it involved large samples of students.

Usually during focus groups students were asked to talk about their classroom experiences, whether they felt teachers treated students 'fairly', and about experiences related to their identified vulnerability, such as missing lessons, being overlooked, or disaffected. These groups sometimes comprised the target students only, while on other occasions they were a randomly chosen group, or mixtures of both targeted and non-targeted students. Focus groups sessions were routinely recorded – via note taking or a digital recorder – and usually the recordings were transcribed so all of the school project team could access them.

Involving students directly

As the data collection activities continued, it became increasingly evident that the most powerful challenges were emerging from the views of students. This being the case, towards the end of the second year some of the staff teams became interested in the idea of involving students more actively in processes of inquiry. As a result, during the following year we introduced a programme of cross-school workshops that prepared students to undertake inquiries in their schools, which was repeated in each subsequent year. These workshops were attended by teams of six students from each of the schools involved. Student teams attended the workshops with a member of staff from the school who, to varying degrees, joined in the activities. (Figures 5.1 and 5.2 show activities at one of these events.)

Figure 5.1 Students working in cross-school groups

Figure 5.2 Students reviewing their discussions at a workshop

Typically the workshops brought together forty to fifty students who were introduced to various strategies for collecting and recording data. During the workshops they used some of these strategies to gather information about one another and to experience what it feels like to be involved in research. In addition, they discussed questions being addressed by staff in their schools: the meaning of fairness, and their experiences of 'fairness' or otherwise during their schooling. These students then returned to their schools and, with the support of their teachers and the university team, carried out inquiries into the views of fellow students in their own schools. Later, they reported back their experiences and findings at a further cross-school workshop and, in some cases, at the network's annual staff conference.

What was clear from these gatherings was that students had strong views as to what was fair and unfair in their schools. For example, reference was made to factors such as reward systems, the use of praise, getting noticed and working in groups. On the other hand, unfairness was said to be reflected in bullying, favouritism, teachers focusing on the badly behaved students, 'naughty' students disrupting lessons, boring lessons, copying from books, being 'picked on' by teachers, not being able to get away from a 'bad reputation' within a school, the use of whole class detentions and not being given support to catch up when lessons were missed through no fault of their own.

What energised the students most, however, was how similar their experiences were, given that they felt that they came from such different schools. For example, a student from a school with a poor reputation commented:

> You know, like, we're stereotyped as the really bad school, but actually we've all got the same problem, got similar problems to what we have. We knew we wouldn't be the only school, but not that they all have similar problems or on the same scale.

Overwhelmingly, the key aspect that the students enjoyed most from being involved in the workshops was meeting students from other schools in order to discuss their ideas and opinions. They were occasionally surprised to find that some students from other schools lived very close to them – reminding us, of course, of the extent of the mobility across Stockborough schools. However, students from one of the underperforming schools commented that some students from the other schools were 'too pushy', and these students seemed reluctant to continue their involvement. This group of students was somewhat quieter and more wary of talking openly to outsiders than their peers.

Unfortunately, not all the student teams managed to carry out inquiries in their own schools. Those that did focused on questions such as: What makes a lesson fair? Are lessons in this school fair? What can we do about low level disruption? Why do some students behave badly? How much do students feel

part of a group in our school, and part of school? In most instances, the investigations that were conducted led to students making presentations to their peers
and school staff.

Making sense of the data

The data collected using the various methods we have described was usually
shared with members of the staff inquiry teams to provide them with access
to students' views, and thus encourage transparency and trust. These accounts
also enabled teams to hold more informed discussions, interpreting the data
themselves, rather than having it interpreted for them and reported back by
external researchers. Names were removed, to avoid finger-pointing and maintain confidentiality, but also to create a body of data about student experience
that, potentially, became the responsibility of all staff members in the school.
Scrutinising the accounts, the teams and members of the university group
together identified 'chunks' of dialogue, or quotes from the student data, that
'jumped out', or made them stop and think. This process was usually repeated
several times, until finally the transcripts were condensed into a number of dialogue extracts, organised by themes that could then be used as starting points
for wider staff discussion in the school. Sometimes the boundary between
research and reflective practice became blurred as the process of engaging with
data stimulated further professional debate.

In one case, Year 8 student responses to a questionnaire about how they
felt about their everyday experiences at school were rather bland and relatively
positive in terms of the numbers circled in the choice of responses provided.
However, boxes were provided underneath these responses where students
were encouraged to write about their feelings. One teacher commented, 'and by
God they did, with a vengeance.' She added:

> It was as if in those written responses, for the first time, they had been
> given this voice. Looking at the questionnaire it was not just looking at
> what was written, it was also the handwriting and how that biro had been
> wielded like a sword and the papers were gouged. These are children who
> never get detentions, who never rock the boat, who never want to be seen
> or heard, but they were going at this paper.

School change as a micro-political process

As we took part in and observed these inquiry-based activities we were regularly reminded that things were going on in the background – mainly in
our absence – that were influencing the way the project evolved in particular contexts. Drawing on the second of House's perspectives, we realised

that these involved micro-political processes of various kinds, within which those involved struggled – and sometimes fought – to determine priorities for action. We suspected, too, that these struggles might sometimes involve other stakeholders within the schools whose priorities were different to those with which the project was concerned. Our partial involvement was slightly frustrating in this respect, often leaving us to speculate about what was happening 'off-stage'. In what follows we touch briefly on some examples of micro-political factors we became aware of, though doubtless there were others that we missed.

The status of the school teams

Our assumption was that the inquiry teams would be seen as temporary structures, set up to lead development on behalf of the whole school community. In practice, the degree to which this was possible seemed to depend on a series of factors, not least the extent to which the team had access to key decision-makers within the school.

In one of the schools, Central High, the way in which membership of the team was determined created obvious difficulties in this respect. The tradition in the school was that all staff had to choose something from a range of professional activities being offered each year, one of which became the 'Equity Research Project'. Staff members were expected to devote 90 minutes each month of their directed time to engage in their chosen activity. The four who opted to be involved in the equity project, were the head of English, a science teacher and two teaching assistants. The assistants were well educated but, for various reasons, had come into working in schools relatively late in their lives and had no formal teaching qualifications. They mainly supported students with English as an additional language. It concerned us that none of the group was from the senior leadership team, nor were any of them of Asian heritage, even though most of the student population was.

We observed that this team was relatively slow in moving forward with its inquiries. As a result, we offered additional support in an effort to help them to take action, initially taking on responsibility for data gathering activities. In discussion, members of the staff team explained that they did not feel that they had sufficient access to the decision-making processes to gain support to carry out their inquiries. When challenged, the head teacher refuted this, saying the staff could come and ask him for support at any time.

We remained unconvinced that this would happen, not least because of what we saw as the rather hierarchical relationships that existed within the school. For example, members of staff always referred to the head by his surname, suggesting a level of formality and distance between them. A similarly deferential approach also appeared to exist within the team. The two teaching assistants both said that they felt they could not make any decisions or take action without first consulting the two teachers, and added that their status in the school was very low. At the end of their first year, the team also commented that they felt like 'a secret society', since they had no means of sharing their findings with others in the school.

This staff team talked much more than others about how the lack of time was a hindering factor in developing their inquiry. Indeed, they became resentful of the amount of time it was taking up. They had expected that they would be able to do it in their specified professional development time, but somehow this had not been the case.

These difficulties appeared to be acknowledged, and in the subsequent years of the school's involvement a deputy head teacher took on the task of coordination, with an administrator looking after communication and coordination activities. Changes in membership were also made in order to improve the group's status. As a result, a significant increase in impact was noted after the first year.

Elsewhere, a striking and positive feature of development in a number of the schools was the way that involvement in SERN opened up opportunities for professional and, indeed, career development for members of staff. This was most evident at events within schools and at cross-schools meetings, when relatively junior people were seen to take on leadership roles. Sometimes this would mean that they were effectively coordinating the work of colleagues who were senior to them.

Senior staff in some of the schools seemed to see the potential of this. So, for example, the head of Moorside selected a newly appointed young advanced skills teacher (AST) to lead the project. He had been appointed with a specific remit to improve teaching and learning across the curriculum and, although not officially a senior leader, he seemed to act as one. The head also selected two teaching assistants, both of whose children had attended the school. Neither of them had formal qualifications but one had started to do a part-time degree and was keen to move on in her teaching career. They were both clearly loyal to the school, committed to the students, and heavily involved in the pastoral and behavioural aspects of the students' experiences. In addition, the head selected a long-standing, well-liked and senior member of staff, and a newly appointed assistant head. However, within three months both these members had dropped out because of other commitments. Throughout the project the AST and the two teaching assistants remained as core team members.

The team met fairly regularly in the learning support unit, where one of the teaching assistants was based. Initially it seemed difficult for them to pull together. However, they seemed to gel once some of the members had left.

Despite the AST often providing typed-up notes of action plans, it rarely felt as if he was leading the meetings, although our sense was that he was quietly moving things along. Everyone chipped in and the team members, regardless of roles in school, suggested ideas and volunteered actions. They took it in turns to coordinate activities and communications, joking that it was perhaps not wise to leave these activities to the AST. However, he coordinated the main research activities and the whole school events. By the end of the year the team was meeting on a weekly basis after school, and they admitted that sometimes this was partly social, as they enjoyed each other's company.

There was, we felt, a sense of mutual respect within the group. This was never more evident than when they were preparing for an important whole school workshop, and the AST was adamant that everyone involved should speak, because 'everyone has done loads'. He was also quite protective of the team, saying that he would present any 'difficult bits' – by which he meant anything controversial. Similarly, at cross-school meetings the team members took it in turns to speak for their team. In effect, the AST's approach spread his own status to colleagues' contributions, which was good for individual development. Although this might also be regarded as an indication of the lingering influence of patronage, it was obvious that the team members had genuine mutual respect for each other.

Changing membership

As we have noted, over the five years of our involvement, schools moved in and out of the network. In all, fourteen out of a possible sixteen high schools were involved at various stages. One was involved for all of these five years, three for four years, three for three years, four for two years and four for one year. One school joined for one year, left and then re-joined after a break of two years. In the main, the schools took up a new investigation in each year of their involvement, although there was often a degree of overlap.

The written agreement with schools stated that researchers from the Centre for Equity in Education would work with school inquiry teams in each of the schools 'in developing, implementing and evaluating plans' for addressing the SERN agenda in ways that were relevant to particular contexts. As outlined in Chapter 3, this proposal stated that the teams would comprise 'five or six staff members representing different perspectives within their school communities', and that one member from each team would be from the senior leadership team to enable access to resources. They would work closely together throughout the year on their inquiries into equity. It was left up to the head teacher to decide how to select the team and the proposal also stated that the heads would continue to have an 'active role' in supporting the team once established.

As it turned out, the membership of these teams and, indeed, the ways in which they carried out their tasks varied considerably from school to school, and to a lesser extent within the schools if they were involved for more than one year. How the teams were selected, how they developed, how they related to other staff in their schools and the nature of the head's involvement seemed to reflect the different traditions of each school.

We saw, too, how changing circumstances, not least as a result of pressures from national policies, led to team membership changing quite regularly. So, for example, at Valley High the assistant head who coordinated the team explained how she and the head teacher selected the team members. They invited people who they felt shared the 'inclusive values' underpinning the network and who could lead developments within the school, but who also between them had a range of roles, skills, experiences and perspectives. Apart from the assistant head, the selected team comprised a senior leader, an advanced skills teacher (AST) in science (who was also doing a PhD in Education), a core-subject teacher, the head of Year 10 and a teaching assistant who acted as the school's inclusion manager.

They were all sent a carefully worded letter, on official school paper, inviting them to join the team to help improve equitable provision, and stating that they had been selected because of their outstanding contribution to the school and their potential for leadership. They were also told they would be working with researchers from the University of Manchester – including an 'eminent professor' – and that their work could have national and international implications. Not surprisingly, they all accepted. However, by the beginning of term the head of Year 10 had been told to leave the team to focus on raising attainment levels, since GCSE results had dropped in the summer exams, leading to the school dropping three places in the local school league table. The core-subject teacher also left soon after for maternity leave.

Despite these unanticipated changes, the team appeared to work well together. At the first meeting they all seemed to participate enthusiastically and were able to question each other comfortably. Back in school, they started their inquiries by each observing three different students in several lessons, writing up their summaries, sharing these between them, and then meeting to discuss their findings. Everyone was involved and there was a sense that everyone had something of value to contribute. The assistant head orchestrated the whole activity but made sure everyone had a voice. At subsequent meetings about other activities, the AST became increasingly vocal and eloquent. Nevertheless, the others continued to contribute in terms of carrying out the activities.

By the second half of the year, it was clear that the AST and assistant head were fronting the inquiry. This led the teaching assistant to express concerns about her role in the team. She said that as the only 'non-teaching colleague' she felt she did not have enough 'authority to convince the cynics', adding that she felt out of her depth, and that the senior leader shared similar feelings. She explained that working in the team had been 'interesting' because before then one of the teachers in the team had not 'acknowledged her presence', despite her supporting students in his lessons and often seeing him round the school. By the end of the year the AST had won a grant to develop further some of the inquiry activities, as part of continuing professional development in the school.

By the second year, both the senior leader and teaching assistant had left the team and some new teachers joined. The assistant head was still coordinating activities but it became clear that she was unable to focus for much of the year because of personal issues related to family illness. At the same time, the AST wanted to remain in the team to report back on his professional development project, even though he now seemed reluctant for the other members of the team to be directly involved. Consequently, they decided that they would each conduct their own individual inquiries. Inevitably, this led to fragmentation of effort and the activities of the team floundered. Subsequently, a new team was formed but they seemed to find it hard to find time to work on the inquiries together.

These examples – and there were several others during the five years – underline that, as Collins (2001) points out, if you hope to reach the right destination, you have to 'get the right people on the bus', and keep them there. It is hard, as outsiders, to know whether or not in selecting their teams, schools were conscious that who was included would carry important messages to the staff as whole about how senior management prioritised the project. But conscious or not, it was clear that the status and micro-political influence of team members had as much impact on what schools did with the outcomes from the inquiries as what these inquiries revealed.

School change as a process of re-culturing

Moving to the third of House's perspectives on innovation, our knowledge of research on organisational change and school improvement led us to recognise that as we engaged with our colleagues we were stepping into contexts that each had their own organisational histories (e.g. Schein, 1985; Hopkins *et al.*, 1994). We also knew that such histories create particular ways of thinking and behaving that can be said to be indicative of the culture of the school (Hargreaves, 1995). In analyses of schools, much of this is taken for granted and unstated, even though research suggests that it has profound effects on the way members of the school community conduct themselves and carry out their day-to-day tasks. This being the case, the ultimate goal of improvement efforts, particularly those that are driven by a strong commitment to particular value positions, must be to infiltrate and, if possible, make changes in a school's culture.

The largely taken-for-granted impact of organisational culture on norms and behaviour makes it difficult for external researchers to analyse and make sense of what they involve, how they are created and how they can be changed (Schein, 1985). Nevertheless, we were conscious that we were engaged in a process which would be influenced by and exert influence on existing norms in the schools.

Cultural resistance

The ways of working we were seeking to encourage, by implication, required changes in school organisation in order that the staff teams could carry out their tasks. Such changes inevitably come up against cultural norms within a school, in one way or another.

As we have seen, for the teams, even finding time to get together within the busy schedule of a secondary school was an ongoing challenge. This meant that adequate time to discuss plans and findings, and decide actions to be taken was always going to be difficult within the school day. The selection of team members who got on well and had a strong sense of commitment to one another or to the task could be helpful in this respect.

We saw an example of this at Highlands, where a group of staff was selected to coordinate the network activities by the head teacher because they already existed as 'the inclusion team'. As such, their work within the network was directly related to their day-to-day roles in the school and finding time to meet was therefore likely to be less of a problem. All the teacher members had middle or senior management positions. They talked very openly and excitedly about their activities in the school, and it was clear that the existing relationships and habits of this 'subcultural' grouping reinforced the collective energies with which they approached the SERN. The senior member of the group, the deputy head, emerged as being 'in charge', especially at cross-school meetings, where she would generally act as the spokesperson for the team, but this too reinforced existing norms and authority patterns.

In the second year, however, the deputy became acting head and so left the team. A new coordinator was identified, and team business became very much more formal. Instead of fitting in meetings and finding opportunities to work on the project during their normal work patterns, times when the team would meet were incorporated into the school diary, up to a year in advance. These meetings became increasingly formal and occasionally minuted, with team members having to account for their actions or lack of them since the previous meeting. As well as the tensions this change in culture created within the team, it seemed there were also tensions between some individual team members about their respective responsibilities regarding inclusion policy.

Even by the end of the third year – and despite a considerable amount of activity – the team had not actively reported to others in the school on their findings and some colleagues commented that they felt like they had become 'a secret society'. Eventually, this came to a head when a senior member of staff from outside the team 'accused' them of making no progress in resolving the equity issues they had investigated. For her, it seemed, these issues were solely the responsibility of the inquiry team, whereas the team members were frustrated at their inability to develop the work and spread it into a whole school strategy to reduce inequities.

What we see here is that the wider school culture was insulated from the project through the way it was managed – as a result, any changes were limited to the group directly involved. Looking inside this group, initially the work of the project seemed stimulating and it complemented the existing cultural norms of collaboration and collective responsibility. However, changes within the group, and other changes imposed on its members, were at odds with these norms – essentially working on the project required staff to alter the way they normally worked with their colleagues. As a result, the project became a source of disagreements and irritation, undermining the positive culture that had previously been sustained.

The frustrating experiences of Highlands point to what was a major challenge for most of the school teams: how to translate their findings into some form of action to bring about school-wide changes in practice. Inevitably, this cannot be done without altering cultural norms. In some cases these norms were experienced as hidden barriers that prevented real changes from taking place, even when there was a rhetoric that suggested a school would adapt practices in the light of the findings.

So, for example, the team at Long Road knew that the evidence they had gathered through questionnaires, focus groups and photo-voice from so-called wallpaper students was 'sensitive stuff' to relay to the rest of the staff. Nevertheless, they felt they had a responsibility to do something. They wanted their colleagues to understand how the team had gathered these data and what it had to say to them, as they felt this would increase empathy with students and encourage colleagues to be more tolerant. However, they were especially sensitive since the school was soon to close and many of their colleagues felt insecure about their futures.

During one staff development session, they asked all of the staff to complete a similar questionnaire to the one given to the students. The responses were mixed, with one colleague commenting that he/she sometimes felt like a 'wallpaper teacher', rarely getting recognition. Having read several comments like this, the team felt that the issue of staff and their relationships with the children was 'a much bigger and complex situation' than previously considered. As one teacher explained, they felt that '*[they could not] have equity for the children without equity for the staff*'. The feeling was that the relationship between these two problems was so 'intermeshed' that they could not address one without addressing the other. Here the team made a difficult but important discovery about the indivisibility of organisational culture: it is most unlikely that the student culture in a school can be altered while the staff culture remains the same, however attractive the idea may seem.

Relationships between students and staff were also a feature at Valley High when the staff embarked on an initiative to explore aspects of their practice based on the lesson study approach we described in Chapter 2. This involved trios of teachers observing students in each other's lessons, and then reflecting on the learning experience together. By the end of the year, the students being observed had become directly involved in the process. Using a traffic light system (green, amber, red) the students showed coloured cards indicating how they felt about different stages of the lesson to an observing teacher sitting at the back of the lesson. The teachers and students then had lunch together to discuss the results.

Over the following two years, the staff found that the absolute imperative for students was their relationship with the teacher. So, while much attention was given to classroom organisation and teaching approaches, what appeared to make the difference was the quality of the relationship between student and teacher. It became evident, however, that the direct involvement of students in these inquiries had the potential to be problematic in terms of school norms. Indeed, in one school, some of the inquiry team were reluctant to encourage students to take part in classroom observations, since they felt this might lead some of their colleagues to involve their professional associations. In another school, when staff presented students' views at a school meeting, a number of their colleagues felt uncomfortable about the findings and angry with the teachers involved for using students' views in such a way. This reminds us of another problem encountered when trying to change schools: even changes that manifestly improve the quality of student experience may be resisted if they disturb the current behaviours and norms of some teachers.

Cultural adjustment

Without changes in those factors – values, norms, behaviours – that underpin organisational culture, even enforced change cannot be sustained. Gradually, in some of the schools at least, we did see adjustments in school cultures that were prompted by the activities of the staff teams. In these contexts, the processes of inquiry were themselves most often the key to change. One teacher from Valley High explained:

We moved into the first year of SERN trying to find some answers. We had some crisp questions and we wanted to collect some numbers, analyse the outcomes and to be able to say 'and here's what we found out'.

The staff felt that the important outcomes of their inquiries related to the things that teachers do 'in particular lessons at particular times' which appeared to build successful learning relationships with targeted students. However, having reflected on what had happened, one of the team concluded that, for her, the more significant outcome was that *'what we started to do was develop some processes, and those processes are now spreading into the wider school development activities'*.

The developments in some of the schools confirmed our experience from earlier projects that opportunities for staff to see one another at work can, under the right conditions, lead to significant changes in professional relationships which, in turn, lead to changes in individual and group behaviour. There was also evidence that such relationships can encourage the sharing of expertise and stimulate individual change. For example, at one point team members from several schools were inspired by a visit to a school in another local authority. In that school, all members of teaching staff were organised into trios from different disciplines who peer-mentored one another by planning, observing and discussing lessons together. Encouraged by what he had seen, a teacher from one school asked for volunteers to work in a similar experiment. The initial round of observations immediately led to debates about the extent to which particular students were participating and learning during the lesson. During a second round of observations, the volunteers decided to repeat the process, but this time to ask students from their target group what they felt about the lesson and what they felt they were learning.

The discussions with the students seemed to indicate that what kind of activity was going on – whether it involved group work, practical tasks, discussions or even copying from the board – was of secondary importance. Once again, what emerged was that the most important factor associated with learning was their relationship with the teacher. Reflecting on these experiences, the teacher who led this initiative commented:

> It has been a real eye-opener, especially in our school where we focus a lot on teaching approaches, methods and techniques, and on classroom organisation. But it appears that what makes the difference is the quality of the relationship and the level of mutual respect, trust and security the student feels with regard to the teacher.

This experimentation proved to be a powerful force for change – powerful enough to trigger the sort of rethinking about roles and behaviours that enable changes in school culture. One teacher who had been involved commented:

We thought we were looking for approaches – classroom organisations, methodologies . . . but these don't appear to have been so important. What has emerged is the strength of relationships. There is nothing really surprising about this, it is just it is not given the priority it perhaps deserves. It is not so much about the three-part lesson, interactive white boards, exam schemes, which text books you are using, assessment processes or anything like that. There are more fundamental issues around social cohesion and what both students and teachers come willingly to school for.

This captures neatly how being able to look at familiar activities and interactions from an unfamiliar perspective – and being able to do this in a context where others are doing the same and are talking about it – can change individuals. The act of inquiring inevitably leads to new knowledge and understandings that cannot be 'unlearnt', thus participation is most often a pathway to acceptance.

A sense of cultural adjustment was also apparent at Moorside, where involvement in SERN was seen by the head as a method of reinforcing morale and commitment during a period of considerable turbulence. As we have mentioned, the school had been in difficulties for many years and, finally, in 2009, it closed. During its final two years, changes introduced through the team's inquiries were used to inform wider developments in the school. One teacher explained:

It is as if the process we went through last year has been taken on board by the whole school, by everybody . . . . It seems reasonable to suggest that the processes set in place by SERN have fed into and had some impact on them.

Members of the project team believed that, through the school's involvement in the network, teachers had gathered strength from working collaboratively in a context that had previously been marked with disputes and divisions. It was important, too, that collaboration involved support staff as well as teachers. Indeed, one teacher commented that *'support staff are integral in this'*, adding that they had *'as valuable an input to make as teachers'*, since they saw *'a much wider range of lessons than most teachers do'* and they tended *'to be closer to the students' experiences of learning'*, especially those students who were difficult or in some way marginalised. He added that they needed *'to draw from as wide and diverse a range of opinion as possible'* in order to increase their understanding of the learning needs of these students. It is a sad fact that the school culture had never been more cohesive and more closely aligned with student needs than it was in the last couple of years before closure. Clearly, a number of factors contributed to this, but there was little doubt among staff members that the work of the SERN project team within the school was one of these.

We also saw evidence of what we took to be changes in culture in Castle, the special school that took part in the network, although this process evolved over a number of years. During the first year the team comprised two long-standing senior managers, two relatively inexperienced teachers, and two learning mentors. During this phase our impression was that there was a degree of complacency in the group. We noticed that the senior teachers, in particular, already felt strongly that the school responded appropriately and effectively to student needs as best they could, and that any inequities related to resources they did not have, rather than practices or attitudes.

Citing 'busy timetables', teaching staff decided that a learning mentor would be able to coordinate and develop the in-school inquiries and organise the team meetings. It struck us that the team was wary of introducing into these activities anything that might be construed as a criticism of existing practice in the school. As a result, beyond celebrating what was already being done, little progress was made.

However, in the second year a younger, less experienced team was put in place, and the head teacher also became a member. Initially, they too chose to investigate an issue that was beyond the school's immediate influence (i.e. the limited opportunities available for disabled students post-school). Predictably, although passionate about this issue, it was difficult for them to have any impact on systems beyond the school. Nevertheless the process of working together seemed to give the team members a sense of their own capacity to do things that would make a difference.

During the following years, the team looked at practices within school and became more critical in their approach. This seemed both to strengthen their resolve and promote new ways of working. One of them commented that there had, in the past, been a divide in the staffroom between the 'old guard', who felt *'that they knew everything'*, and the younger less experienced staff members. But managing the in-school inquiries and implementing changes in response to what these revealed was emancipatory; the status and influence of these younger colleagues grew visibly, leading to a fundamental shift in staff-room and wider school cultures.

The head teacher of Castle was from the outset a particularly strong supporter of the SERN initiative, advocating it to other schools in the area. However, in the beginning his support was possibly driven by a desire to see a general reduction in inequities within local schools, rather than the belief that his own school needed to consider this. On one occasion, he commented that, for him, involvement was the *'icing on the cake'*, the implication being that it was a small luxury added to an already successful recipe. However, after listening to some of his colleagues present accounts of their work at the fourth annual SERN conference he announced, *'I now realise – this is the cake'*. This was a clear and, for us, significant indication of the cultural shift that was taking place within the school community.

Culture and leadership

It has been argued that organisational culture and leadership are two sides of the same coin (Schein, 1985). If this is so, it is not surprising that, throughout the project, the role of head teachers regularly came into the spotlight. During the first phase, in particular, the head teachers' commitment to cross-school collaboration was strongly stated. However, as we note in Chapter 2, our experience in earlier initiatives suggested that such commitment was not always translated into actions, often leaving staff groups feeling unsupported.

We were convinced that within the SERN schools, the attitudes and actions of head teachers would be central to meaningful progress, not least through the authority and resources they were prepared to delegate to their project teams. Early signs were encouraging. We saw, for example, how the head of Valley, who had only been in post for a short time, was prepared to challenge the school's embedded cultural practices, especially with regard to inclusion. The assistant head, who was project coordinator, appeared to hold views very similar to those of the head, and their joint energies promised a powerful force for change.

The head was very supportive of the project group's activities and this was made clear to the whole staff by his readiness to allow them to take lesson time to observe other teachers' teaching, to hold a meeting about project planning with the full senior leadership team (to which university researchers were invited), and to enable the team to organise a whole-school workshop to which governors were also invited. These meetings were challenging and raised sensitive questions about the quality of teaching and learning in the school. The head used the discussions to explore ideas about areas where changes were needed in the school.

By the second year, however, the head appeared to have shifted the focus of his attention elsewhere, reminding us that externally driven policy imperatives can change priorities, even amongst those who were strongly committed to the work of the network. His capacity to preach the power of the teacher-led inquiry was not diminished, however, as was obvious in staff meetings, yet we sensed that the moment had passed and that teachers in the school knew this.

This head teacher continued to be a key contributor at the heads' meetings, maintaining his support for the network as a whole and often speaking eloquently about the network at the secondary heads meetings, which probably inspired some other heads to join the project in subsequent years.

Nevertheless, when we proposed that the network should take collaboration a stage further, by conducting cross-school inquiry activities, he was the first to say his school was not ready for this. Again, we were reminded that often when heads 'welcome' challenge, they welcome it on their own terms.

Other head teachers had been less willing to voice commitment to the network. For example, at one quite memorable meeting, one of the original group of heads explained that his school participated only because he supported the collaborative spirit expressed through the setting up of a network – beyond that, he did not really value it. Regarding the specific needs of his school, he saw the project team's activities as peripheral to his improvement plan for the school. He also commented on another occasion that, as it happened, the teachers who had volunteered to be part of the inquiry team themselves displayed limited understanding of equity issues, and he hoped participation in the project might broaden these understandings.

In another school, Highlands, the head appeared to be passionate about the network's purposes, and he too argued eloquently for more equitable provision. He also gave support to his team, who clearly valued his enthusiasm and encouragement. However, he left the school after the first year of its involvement and over the next three years the school had a procession of acting head teachers. It was difficult for any of these heads to maintain this support in any meaningful way, though the project team continued, perhaps creating a further source of friction in an already struggling school.

The team at Moorside High was also very aware of the head teacher's support and, indeed, his trust. On several occasions he advised colleague heads to 'stand back' and let the teams develop their own inquiries. In his own school, not only did he give the project team a free hand, he also enabled access to resources and made it clear that the team were doing important work and enjoyed his confidence. On more than one occasion he commented that the team played a crucial role in moving the school forward. As he saw it, while he represented the hard-line, 'top-down' approach, the team was more 'grass-roots', demonstrating that change was not just being imposed from above but was also driven by staff not normally seen as working with the senior leadership team.

In all of these instances, it was clear that what head teachers did or did not do proved central to the success of the project teams. It seems that the heads were acting as gatekeepers – sometimes prompting changes in practice, sometimes allowing it, and sometimes preferring what Handy (1991) has referred to as a 'procedural illusion of change', rather than change itself. In every case, we can see that while change can be initiated at many levels in the school, if can generally be either sanctioned or blocked from the top.

Towards a collective culture

The new relationships that were created between colleagues across the different schools created a further dynamic. Our assumption was that this would provide opportunities for professional learning and cross-school developments, as we had witnessed in earlier projects. However, the development on this front was quite limited, despite the commitment to collaboration articulated by many of the head teachers.

Nevertheless, we did witness the gradual strengthening of trust and professional respect between inquiry team members from the different schools. In particular, occasions that involved the different teams working collaboratively as critical friends to one another's inquiries seemed to create a sense of mutuality and certainly built some strong personal links. In these contexts, participants seemed to recognise that – regardless of their school, status or roles – they were engaged in a common journey. At its best, such activity could facilitate lateral and diagonal learning within the wider group, and these shared experiences certainly helped to 'glue' the network together.

Occasionally new ideas were generated through the coming together of different perspectives. Further, during cross-school activities, we witnessed many examples of participants learning from and supporting one another, as they reflected on and adapted ideas and practices. Sometimes, we saw that this enabled risk-taking, as colleagues presented their findings and floated ideas at potentially challenging meetings. As one teacher commented, *'I think that knowing that other schools are working on this has helped us be more bold, more daring in our thinking'*. Collaboration also helped to create an 'impetus' to get things done, described by another teacher as stemming from the knowledge that they would have to *'present ourselves'* in some way at cross-school meetings, even though these seemed relaxed and informal gatherings.

These experiences lead us to conclude that collaboration around common challenges and teacher interactions across schools can create a sense of local responsibility and agency. Discussions around the findings of the various school teams seemed to operate at two levels. On the one hand, they provided insights into the varied and complex organisational cultures within which teachers work; for example, one teacher reported feeling 'inspired' by another team's success in engaging with and developing the project in a very difficult context. On the other hand, within this variation, there was nevertheless a sense of resonance in that – despite contextual differences – there was considerable similarity in the students' experiences within the different schools. It was also clear that all schools fail some students, no matter how 'good' they are.

The schools increasingly wanted to conduct more cross-school activities and often team members aired their dissatisfaction with the way provision for students was organised at the local level. This led one teacher to argue that it *'shouldn't really matter which school they go to, they are all equally deserving. . . . I now feel that I have a responsibility to all students in [the area]'.*

The role of the university team

At this point it is worth noting that our own involvement in the schools was in itself a new factor within the internal politics of these communities. Our aim was to develop effective working relationships with our school partners in order to bring together the different expertise of practitioners and academics. In doing this we drew on our experiences in previous collaborative projects, but inevitably most of the staff involved in most of the schools had no such experience to draw on. Nevertheless, we were particularly keen to ensure that SERN was neither described nor thought of as a university activity in which some schools and teachers were involved. Rather, from the outset it was to be an activity driven by the schools – each of which was conducting its own individual project within a wider local initiative, which university researchers would support, where possible, but could not lead.

Many participants commented that their feelings of ownership about the project had contributed significantly to their motivation and sense of empowerment. The inquiry approach gave team members flexibility to think about how to take their projects forward in relation to areas of focus that emerged from their own investigations and data. The university team clearly played some role here, for example advising on data collection methods when asked, and participating in the sense-making discussions where appropriate, but all the time making it clear that the project teams must think of themselves as the 'experts' when it came to understanding what was happening and deciding what needed to be done in their own schools. At least some of those participating found this relationship different from expectations; for example, one teacher commented:

> It's non-threatening. I don't get the impression that you're critical of us. I found it very supportive. You've come up with suggestions and things without telling us this is what we should be doing.

Another teacher explained how this looked from her perspective:

> The project's very different in the way that it's structured, in that we chose what it was we were looking at, what it was we were researching, how we were going to move forward.

Similarly, a teacher in another school also emphasised the importance of ownership:

It's very much our project and relevant to our school. We've got to have complete ownership of it and believe in it in order for us to go on . . . eventually we're going to have to go and sell some of these things to colleagues within the school and if we don't believe in it, or if we're just sort of going through the motions because we have to or we've been told to . . . well . . .

On the other hand, some staff found the absence of clear goals and predetermined steps set for them rather frustrating. However, as one teacher reflected, in contrast, implementing external programmes (national strategies were cited) can feel '*soulless*', and another added, '*it's not just another working party we do to tick a box or something to impress Ofsted*'.

At the same time many of the school teams commented on the importance of having some form of external impetus to keep them focused and to provide support. One teacher noted that other initiatives tend to be '*full-on at the beginning, all singing and dancing, and then it's sort of . . . never monitored again*'. A participant explained the significance of this role as being '*more to sort of keep us focused, sort of write things up when you know we've scrawled things on pieces of paper, keep us on track, keep the momentum going, make us sort out meetings and liaisons with other schools*'.

Conclusion

So, what can we draw from our analysis of what happened within the schools that took part in the network? What does this tell us that would be valuable of others wishing to use inquiry-based approaches to the development of more equitable schools?

On the positive side there is much that offers reasons for optimism. Many of the schools did find ways of overcoming the challenges of finding the time and mobilising human resources in order to collect and engage with evidence regarding groups of learners seen as being vulnerable within existing school arrangements. We also saw the way staff teams developed innovative ways of collecting the views of the students themselves. And, as we have explained, this often stimulated debate and reflection, leading to serious efforts to move school policies and practices in a more equitable direction.

There is, however, a more negative set of issues that emerge from our analysis. These point to the ways in which structural factors within schools, some of which relate to the external policy context, limit opportunities for using such approaches. We have also provided a sense of how the attitudes of key individuals, and the traditions and cultures within organisations, can create further barriers to progress. Later, in Chapter 7, we look in more detail at these factors, looking specifically at their causes. First of all, however, in the next chapter, we review the impact of the activities that took place.

6   Assessing the impact

So far we have described and analysed some of the complexities of what happened as the staff teams attempted to develop an inquiry-based approach to issues of equity in their schools. In this chapter we consider the impact of their efforts. In so doing, we set out to assess the extent to which the network contributed to the development of equity within the Stockborough secondary schools.

Taking place as it did over a period of five years of intense government activity to improve educational outcomes – or at least raise the annually reported GCSE attainment levels – this was a time of multiple policy initiatives and interventions to drive-up standards. Consequently, it is not always easy to disentangle particular effects and attribute them to the work of the project teams, rather than the pressures imposed generally on schools over this period of time. Nonetheless, as is clearly evidenced by the accounts reported in earlier chapters, teachers in the schools themselves felt able to identify changes and to trace these to their involvement in the SERN project.

In considering these changes in more detail we set out to assess the impact of the initiative on the schools, their students and staff. We go on to reflect on what can be learnt from the experiences of these schools during the project, specifically about the empowering of staff-led inquiry groups as a school improvement strategy and, more generally, about achieving more equitable educational provision.

Impact on schools

We do not feel in a position to make any general claims for the impact of SERN on the overall performance levels of the project schools in national examinations. They did improve over the period – in some cases quite sharply – but, as we have noted, there were a number of initiatives taking place during the period and it is not possible to isolate the impact of any one of these. However, it can be asserted that these schools contributed fully to the overall increase in examination results recorded in Stockborough during this period. In fact, the percentage of students gaining five or more A* to C grades at GCSE went up from 54.6 per cent in 2005 to 76.5 per cent in 2010, a rise of 22 per cent (during the same period the national average went from 56.3 per cent to 75.3 per cent, up by 19 per cent). Looking at a more inclusive measure of student performance, during the same period the percentage of Stockborough students gaining five or more A* to G grades went up at almost twice the national average, from 90 per cent to 96.1 per cent (compared to 89 per cent upto 92.7 per cent nationally). Improvement levels within individual schools varied considerably in this dimension. As we have explained, the schools were drawn from a relatively small education district made up of a number of discreet towns and semi-rural areas. These were, to a large extent, separate communities. The schools were also very different in terms of public perceptions of them, with some being seen as 'doing well' and therefore attractive to parents, and others that were much less well regarded and under the threat of imminent closure.

In some ways these differences mediated the impact of national policies: for some these seemed to be prescriptions that had to be swallowed whole, while others could be rather more selective when confronted by national dictates, scaling down or delaying implementation. It is not surprising therefore that in some of the schools, at some times, externally mandated priorities seemed to sweep aside internal policies and plans, as we have detailed in previous chapters. Nevertheless, through our regular contacts with the schools, we were able to monitor the way that the involvement in SERN impacted on the schools, particularly with respect to policies, practices and the processes of networking, and to note certain patterns.

Educational equity as a policy goal

In every case, joining the project triggered a review of current provision in the school to establish how far current policies were delivering equitable opportunities to students. This was accompanied by a clear commitment to create a school community in which 'no student misses out'. Of course, most schools work reasonably well for most of their students; the difficulty is developing a school which works for all learners. However, writing this commitment explicitly into the school's goals, so that it is automatically picked up in development plans, is an important step forward.

Whilst having a policy on equity is a significant starting point, it seemed to us that the real impact came when the commitment began to colonise other strategic decisions. There were clear examples of this happening, such as at Leafy Top High, where during the second year of its involvement a school-wide strategy planting equity firmly into assessment, behaviour and curriculum policies was introduced. These policies were developed through inquiry groups that involved more than half of the teachers in the school. Our observations suggested that these activities had a powerful impact on the ethos and values within the school community.

Similarly, at Castle High – where senior staff believed that equity was already central to the school's values and policies – we saw how teacher-led inquiries gradually provoked a less comfortable picture of the way staff actually carried out their work. As the head teacher articulated, it was not until the third year of involvement that the school 'caught on', realising that they needed to think much more deeply about what equity implied in their particular context.

Policy into practice

Of course, policy is not always reflected in practice, and it is much easier to develop whole school policies than it is to implement them. While there were many examples of project schools genuinely striving to ensure greater equity, it is also the case that all too often within-school activities embraced relatively small groups of staff. In fact, one of the features of the network meetings, especially in the early years, was the way they became a forum for colleagues to share frustrations that their efforts were not being picked up more widely in their own schools. On the one hand, this points to the importance of networking within a school: it is not uncommon for networks to sustain and nourish groups of teachers whose energies may otherwise be depleted by the difficulty of mobilising their immediate colleagues. On the other hand, it reminds us that while we often speak of schools participating in a particular initiative, usually the involvement reaches only part of the school organisation.

Despite these cautions, there seems little doubt that in all of the project schools better understandings of which students were at risk of marginalisation, and how and why this happened, were developed. It is also clear that while these understandings often embraced the hunches that at least some staff members had already, in many instances they also uncovered new and even surprising ways in which some groups of students felt disenfranchised.

Increased networking activity

In some ways, it is helpful to consider the schools as falling into two groups: the original group of four that helped to design the overall approach used within SERN, and those that joined in subsequent years. The original group was characterised by high levels of involvement and enthusiasm amongst the head teachers – for whom equity seemed to be both a conceptual and a practical concern. It struck us that interest in the idea of equity and how this translated into a school setting was both a positive force within the group and, perhaps, a distraction from the practical actions needed to promote equity more broadly within the schools. It was positive because it intrigued the heads and their school team members, and became an important and explicit reason for networking with colleagues from the other schools, at both teacher and head teacher levels.

The clearest example of the way this common conceptual dimension was expressed was the process through which, towards the end of the first year, the schools decided to develop a series of equity indicators. This exercise, which had active participation from all four schools, emerged from a collective review of what the network had achieved during its first year. This review was carried out at a seminar involving the heads and their senior leadership teams. As a result, over the following year, the staff groups from the different schools debated their views on what equitable schooling would look like, and how the degree of equity within a particular school's provision might be assessed using a series of '*indicators*'. There is no doubt that these were stimulating discussions for heads and teachers alike. The head teacher of Central High, in particular, was enthusiastic about this initiative, arguing that it should aim to produce an instrument or a poster that could be used to stimulate a debate regarding equity more widely within schools (see Table 6.1 for the content of the poster that was eventually designed).

At the same time – and despite the importance these discussions had in developing networking activities across the schools – the effort that was put into producing the indicators was probably disproportionate to any practical use to which it could be put. Indeed, as far as we could determine, the value of the discussions that took place was largely restricted to those who were involved in them.

Nevertheless, the process helped to strengthen the sense of collective commitment to the principle of equity and, in so doing, encouraged further support for the work of the network within the four schools. More specifically, the head teachers were able to clarify their own thoughts about what equity is, how it can best be promoted in the school, and so on, in a forum that allowed them both to develop their own thinking, and strengthen relationships and build up trust with their colleagues. Similarly, the school inquiry teams were able to think systematically about what equity looks like in practice and how the degree of equity in current provision might be measured, and to test out their ideas through the development of the indicators. They also came to know their colleagues from the teams in other schools a little more through this process, which certainly strengthened relationships between staff members from different schools.

However, the outcome – the equity indicators themselves – reflect the inevitable contradictions and compromises needed to secure consensus, and though they perhaps held a shared meaning for the groups of teachers who developed them, in practice they represented a fairly blunt audit tool. Indeed, there is an abundance of similar standards, benchmarks and checklists already available, all of which seem heavily influenced by the context in which they were developed. So, the significance resides not in the audit tool produced, which did not even spread with any degree of commitment to schools subsequently joining the project, but in the communication and relationship building that occurred alongside the drawing up of the standards. Consequently we can say that one impact on the schools – at least the first tranche of schools – was increased networking between both head teachers and school project teams.

Unfortunately, this networking activity proved difficult to sustain. In part this was due to the influx of new schools – larger networks are harder to maintain – but also because it proved harder to bring together the head teachers in quite the same way after the first two years of the project. This might be

Table 6.1 The Equity Research Network indicators

In our community we aspire for all to have access, ambition and autonomy. All members of our community:

Access	Ambition	Autonomy
• Feel equally valued and respected for what we do.	• Have high personal goals that we want to achieve.	• Are trusted to make decisions about what subjects we learn and how we learn.
• Take part in equally good quality and varied learning experiences.	• Believe we have the ability and determination to make goals happen.	• Are independent learners so that we are responsible for achieving our goals.
• Have similar facilities to help us do what we want to do.	• Believe the things we learn will help us do what we want to do in the future.	• Show acceptance, understanding, and respect for people who are different in our community.
• Feel equally involved, included, inspired and challenged to learn.	• Feel our family and friends and the local community encourage and support us in what we want to do.	• Take part in making our community a better place for everyone to live.
• Feel our differences are noticed when encouraged and supported to learn.	• Are helped to feel more confident about ourselves.	
	• Believe we can help make the world a better place.	

explained by the schools' histories, in that the original group had a record of previous networking, which was not the case when a wider group of schools joined in. There is also the difference between 'founding' a club and joining one – perhaps the original group felt that they were creating something, while subsequent recruits felt that they were joining someone else's creation, despite the emphasis throughout that the project belonged to member schools. Whatever the reason, the teacher teams continued to report that they both enjoyed the meetings that brought them together with colleagues from other schools and found them quite valuable, but we saw less of the contact and exchange we found amongst the first cohort.

Staff development

The impact on staff was, arguably, the strongest outcome from the SERN initiative. Inevitably, any project that runs over a period of five years will see changes in the personnel involved, and as this project also saw different schools opting in and out at different times, the composition of the staff groups changed each year, sometimes quite substantially. Nevertheless, there was a core of teachers who continued to represent their schools throughout the whole period, who brought continuity to the inquiry groups, and, indeed, to the network meetings and activities. As we monitored what happened, we saw evidence of how their involvement led to changes in their thinking. In particular – and in ways that echoed the arguments that emerged from our earlier research – we saw how an engagement with evidence challenged assumptions, providing new opportunities for professional learning and, in some instances, challenging the status quo in relation to policy and practices within the schools.

Listening and learning

There is no doubt that these teachers were most interested in increasing their knowledge of student attitudes, opinions and responses to their schooling. It should not surprise us that teachers are fascinated by what their students have to say about school, about the teaching they receive and about what they feel helps them most in their learning. Student views about their learning experiences have always had a powerful effect on teachers. Over recent years, the collection of such data has become much more common in schools, as 'student voice' has become an increasingly influential theme in school improvement initiatives (see, for example, Fielding, 2004). Often what these voices tell us seems harsh – students tend to base their views on their received experiences, which are sometimes negative, rather than the plans and motives of their teachers, which are almost universally positive.

An early and striking outcome for teachers from across the SERN schools was that their early hunches and assumptions – their starting points for school-based inquiry – were often not supported by the evidence they collected when they began to investigate the problems they had identified. Of course, hunches are by definition merely best guesses, but the staff groups were nevertheless fairly confident that they knew which students were 'missing out' on schooling. However, as we have seen, in many instances they discovered that teachers' perceptions of problem groups and areas were not as accurate as they imagined. Thus, evidence often challenged existing assumptions about student experience.

So for example, in a couple of schools, it became clear that the students described as 'invisible' were in fact both a larger group and from a much wider ability range than had been assumed; in yet another school, it became clear that assumptions about the needs and priorities of new arrivals to the school did not match the views of the students themselves; elsewhere, the targeting of groups who did not participate in out-of-school activities revealed it was not the range of activities but the perceived attitudes of teachers offering the activities and other students that put students off; while in another school, assumptions about links between gender, ethnicity and disaffection turned out in reality to be more closely associated with the link between literacy levels and disaffection. It also became clear that efforts to improve the experiences of disadvantaged student groups was often hampered, either by difficulty identifying exactly which students belonged to the group, or failure to grasp the source of the disadvantage, or both.

Professional growth

Despite, or perhaps because of these various shocks and surprises, and the consequent undermining of prior assumptions, it was also clear that most teachers who took part felt that they had grown professionally. Interviews with members of the school inquiry teams revealed that, for many of them, participation was a powerful and empowering learning experience.

Some talked explicitly about how they had learnt to identify a problem, investigate it, and then develop and implement a strategy to improve the situation. Most often, this was done in collaboration with colleagues and involved new forms of dialogue with their students. Teachers were able to see the impact of their efforts on the student group, which increased their own levels of satisfaction and motivation. Many of those involved spoke of their sense of personal growth through this experience, and of how it brought home to them that, working together, teachers can make a difference, even in the most difficult of contexts.

Linked to this increased sense of potency, came a parallel deepening of their understanding of teaching as a profession, which seemed to be both exciting and a little worrying. It was worrying because recognising that one can make a difference brings with it a feeling that one should make a difference. It can be exciting because making small differences to students' experiences that can make large differences to their lives is what teaching is about.

This deepening of their understanding of what it means to be a teacher was most obvious where projects engaged directly with the views of students. Fielding (2004) has referred to this as the 'dialogical imperative', and describes it in terms of the obligation that falls on teachers to respond to what students have to say when they have asked them for their opinions. He notes that engaging with student voices can be particularly powerful in changing teachers thinking and practice. Perhaps this is because it is very difficult to dismiss what students tell us – indeed, whatever they say, however hurtful, we can never really say that they are 'wrong'. Rather we must ask why it is that they have negative perceptions of their schooling, despite our best intentions.

Challenging current orthodoxy

Setting out to change practice in schools, even when it has been sanctioned as an 'official' school initiative, will not always be welcomed by those who are required to change. Le Metais (1997) notes that developing more equitable practices often requires the negotiation of a series of tensions under which schools operate; for example, the tension within schools between competing demands and unmet needs. There are no simple formulae that can help us to prioritise some needs over others, which is a recurring problem when needs always exceed the availability of resources. Then there is the tension between curriculum diversity and parity of esteem – it is often difficult to establish that alternative programmes, developed to meet the specific needs of specific groups, are as important in the scheme of things as mainstream, exam-oriented provision.

Such tensions often lead to disagreements between those seeking change and those whose lives will be affected by what is being suggested. This is likely to be exacerbated where those who see the need for change are not in a position to mandate colleagues to comply. This is a problem that many inquiry team members encountered, leading to frustration and even dissatisfaction with school structures and management processes. On many occasions during network meetings, team members shared their frustrations with each other about all of this. Sometimes these related to specific actions that had been blocked or ruled out, more often though they were associated with less dramatic but equally frustrating barriers. Often we heard team members complain, for example, that many colleagues in their own schools did not seem to be aware that there was an initiative to bring about more equitable practice going on in the school. At minimum, they felt that more opportunities to present the findings from their inquiries to colleagues were required.

The work of the inquiry groups

The use of staff inquiry groups as a school improvement strategy is not new. Indeed, as explained in Chapter 2, we ourselves have a long history of association with activities involving such groups. We have documented elsewhere why this seems to be a sensible and practical arrangement for school improvement (Ainscow and Southworth, 1996; Hopkins *et al.*, 1994; West, 1998). Here we use the Stockborough experience to reinforce the advantages of creating such groups as part of a school development strategy.

The number and scope of externally driven changes that have overwhelmed English schools in recent years often seems to generate confusion around priorities and purposes. While we can be sure that this year's policies will be usurped by next year's, governments are generally much less clear about what it is schools can stop doing than what it is they should start doing, or do more of. Over time, this may result in wave after wave of priorities, piled on top of one another, and competing for resources and attention. It is hardly surprising that such circumstances leave many teachers confused about how to prioritise their own time and energies. The first benefit of school inquiry groups is that – for the members at least – it becomes possible to identify clear areas of focus for these efforts, so that they work systematically to achieve defined goals rather than spreading their efforts thinly over too many activities to make much impact on any.

As we note above, empowerment is an important motivator for teachers. The genuine empowerment of groups of teachers in identifying, planning for and implementing school-level strategies to reduce inequities can have a significant impact on the ways they think about themselves and their work. We found, too, that this process can spread beyond the team itself to others who are drawn into its activities, changing communication patterns and influencing decision-making processes. This, in turn, can help to improve the amount and quality of dialogue within schools, encouraging teachers to talk about issues that are fundamental to the processes of education, most often increasing the attention given to learning within discussions of teaching, and increasing the momentum for development. Furthermore, as we saw in previous projects, involving inquiry teams across a network can lead to an increase in the dialogue between schools. In this way, unhelpful competition between schools can be put to one side – at least to some degree – as teachers engage in critical friendship to one another's efforts. In such contexts, we have found that it is common for teachers to discover that they have similar problems and interests, and to build cooperation and trust. Indeed, there was ample evidence that all of these were manifested at various times and in various places during the SERN project.

Looking more closely at the ways the inquiry teams organised themselves within their schools, again we see similarities with our earlier projects. We have previously mapped out the typical stages of development such groups go through (see Table 6.2, adapted from West, 2000).

Initially, there is a tendency for such groups to view their role as essentially a problem-solving task: some aspect of the school is not working as it should and this needs to be put right. We have termed this stage 'delinquency', as the emphasis is most often on corrective strategies. Since the assumption is that existing policies are fine, it is simply a matter of adjusting practice to match these. During this early phase the group is 'forming' and 'norming' (Handy, 1991), establishing roles and relationships, and generally trying to work through existing structures to get things done.

As the process of inquiry takes place we have found that it can be difficult to turn data into information, and information into knowledge (Nonaka and Takeuchi, 1995). At this stage, investigating can become an end in itself, and often little use is made of data that has been gathered, while there is frequent complaining about the lack of resources required to make real improvements. These patterns were apparent in the behaviours of almost all of the SERN inquiry teams during their early involvement, particularly the commitment to 'solve' a particular problem – be it the inclusion of minority students, or the engagement of 'invisible' students.

As the team members move into the second stage, they get to know one another better and become clearer about what they are hoping to achieve. At the same time, attention tends to switch away from eliminating unsatisfactory practice in their own schools, towards importing good practice from elsewhere. Again, this was apparent within SERN, with several instances of schools 'borrowing' practices from one another, as they found out about alternative approaches to common areas of concern. At this stage, the groups were more likely to describe their own deficits in terms of a shortage of ideas and skills rather than resources, and more likely to locate their task within the wider development of the school, rather than see it is a discrete problem with a specific solution. The commitment to network with colleagues across schools strengthened, and those occasions when teams from the various schools came together became more important, with substantial sharing of ideas and approaches and lots of reinforcement to colleagues. The need to change internal structures and procedures within their own schools to facilitate and sustain changes in practice became a frequent topic of conversation, both within and across school groups.

Table 6.2 School inquiry groups: stages of development

Understanding/point of focus for 'task'	Typical attitudes/behaviours	'Solution' linked to
STAGE 1 INTERNAL (Deliquency)	• Uncertainty about focus • Cadre feeling its way • What is 'school improvement'? • What is the role of the cadre group? • How can the cadre group work best together as a group? • Initial reliance on established ways of working • Initial reliance on existing structures • Initial reliance on key personnel/leaders within the cadre • Start to collect data and share it	Resources/attitudes 'Putting things right'
STAGE II EXTERNAL (Opportunity)	• Clearer about focus • Using structures in new ways, e.g. dept. meetings with single item research agendas • New ways of working • Greater openness within the cadre group, e.g. voice of main scale teacher • Better at making meaning from data • Beginning to shift from staff development mode to school improvement mode	Skills/flexibility 'Learning from others'

STAGE III
STRATEGIC
(Utility)
	• Change/renewal of cadre group
	• R & D establishing its own rhythm – SDP becomes more organic
	• New structures emerge – R & D
	• New roles emerge:
	  ◦ HOD as facilitator of research post
	• Establishment of research culture within the school:
	  ◦ Evidence-based
	• Risk-taking
	• Involvement of students (pupils) as researchers:
	  ◦ From data-source to partners in dialogue
	• Collection of date, making meaning and supporting research outcomes
		Ideas/ways of thinking
		Reconceptualising purposes, structures, methods

During the third stage, the groups begin to work more strategically, emphasising analysis rather than description, focusing on implementation strategies and establishing new structures and methods within the school to 'get things done'. At this point there may be changes in team membership, and in the way the group is positioned within the school structure. At the same time, student data are more likely to be seen as a resource within the decision-making process, and there is a growing confidence regarding the collection, analysis and use of student views to improve provision.

This third stage offers the potential that the use of inquiry moves from being a temporary arrangement, used to address a particular concern, towards an approach that becomes embedded in a school's usual way of doing its business. In this way, the school develops a capacity to use inquiry in order to address any new concerns that may emerge and takes on some of the features of what Senge (1989) calls *a learning organisation*, i.e. 'an organisation that is continually expanding its capacity to create its future' (p. 14). Or, to draw on a phrase from Rosenholtz (1989), it becomes a *moving school*, one that is continually seeking to develop and refine its responses to the challenges it meets.

Making schools more equitable

Our consideration of what SERN achieved points to a series of factors that seem to be particularly important for the development of more equitable schools. These relate to attitudes and practices, school access, the curriculum that is provided and the way progress is assessed.

Attitudes and practices

At their most fundamental, the factors we are concerned with are located in classrooms, where, first and foremost, equity is about attitudes. Put simply, the attitudes of teachers – and of fellow students – can either promote or inhibit a fair, welcoming and inclusive working climate. In a school that is committed to fairness, all students should expect to be welcome in their classrooms – not only in explicit ways, which embrace cultural, social and intellectual differences – but also in implicit ways, so they will not feel marginalised because of feedback (or lack of it) on their behaviour and performance. Because all students are welcome, they can expect positive interactions as a normal part of their classroom experience. As a result, they will feel included, valued and acknowledged.

In this sense, language is particularly important because it can be both empowering and disempowering. We were reminded of this when staff at Greenside Grammar presented the results of their investigations into the extent to which sixth form students felt valued and supported. The responses of young people who had transferred to Greenside from other Stockborough schools at the age of sixteen was generally positive. However, many expressed their irritation at being referred to as 'external students', something that shocked the staff, even though they came to realise that this was so obviously a mistake.

Then there is the issue of practice. If teachers favour one style it will tend to most suit those students who are comfortable with that style. In effect, strong teaching orthodoxies can disenfranchise students who are less confident with or less engaged by that approach. Equity therefore requires practitioners who understand the importance of teaching the same thing in different ways to different students, and of teaching different things in different ways to the same students.

The network schools could point to examples of good practice in all of these areas before they joined the project. But the issue they were addressing through their involvement in SERN was whether they were sure that *all* students could feel they were embraced within these ways of working. There are many examples described in earlier chapters which illustrate both that the schools identified groups of students or areas of activity where these expectations were not being met, and that the school then took direct actions to remedy the situation, thereby moving towards more equitable classroom practice. In most of the schools there was evidence, too, of changes in classrooms so that specific groups who were felt to be missing out were now more actively engaged in learning, and this had been achieved through deliberate attention to the attitudes displayed, language used and interactions engineered in lessons, all of which have been reflected in the range of teaching approaches used.

Of course, these are the less difficult aspects of equity to deliver. That is not to deny their value, but simply to accept that while adjustments in classroom practices can have significant impact on the experiences of particular students, they may not do much to alter the factors that led to these students 'missing out' in the first place. Often such factors are more intransigent, and therefore more difficult to influence as a single school.

Access

As we have explained, most Stockborough children attend their nearest school. Unfortunately, proximity tends to segment school populations according to social and economic, and sometimes ethnic and religious factors. Thus we end up with unequal schools – some very much better off in terms of the physical and social capital their students can draw on than others. In effect, this means that, to a large extent, the system draws together students from similar levels of socio-economic background – be it advantaged or disadvantaged – into the same school. Insofar as this is the case, the allocation of students between schools tends to magnify social inequities, and, as we know, social inequities beget educational inequities.

There is, then, an additional complicating factor relating to availability of appropriately qualified staff. Put simply, schools that are perceived to be in difficulties often find it difficult to attract teachers, particularly in certain shortage subjects. So, for example, at one stage, Our Lady's High – a low performing school with the associated challenges – was at crisis point because there were no qualified teachers of mathematics on its staff. Within just a few minutes' walk away – along the same road – were two other secondary schools, one of which was a grammar school, with full teams of suitably qualified teachers. The implication being that the concentrations of disadvantaged learners in particular schools are more often exposed to teaching from inappropriately qualified staff than those in schools serving more privileged groups.

Unless we can find some way to offset the social disadvantage within schools located in less advantaged areas, it will be extremely difficult to establish equitable access through schooling. While individual schools can do little about this on their own, groups of schools working together might be able to produce a fairer system. Through collaboration they might, within given geographical areas, operate access agreements that produce more balanced school populations. Or, they might find ways of pooling their resources – particularly teachers – and using these across a 'family of schools' in order to give support where it is needed and ensure that challenge is built into experience at every level of the system.

Curriculum content

Whilst we assume that all schools set out to provide their students with a curriculum that is relevant to their interests, aptitudes and future lives, in England the national curriculum has made this much more difficult over recent years. While there are some benefits of a common core curriculum – for example, no one would argue with the need for language and communication skills, an understanding of numbers and of the potential of digital technologies – the English national curriculum went well beyond that. When introduced over twenty years ago, it mandated a 100 per cent curriculum model, despite the fact that no one – not even the politicians who introduced it – could seriously believe that there is a single curriculum model that will have equal utility value to all students. Though subsequent governments have relaxed the compulsory elements somewhat over the past twenty years, it is not easy for schools to move away from the model. This is partly because having spent twenty years matching the supply of teachers and school staffing structures to the national curriculum, there is no ready supply of alternative teachers who can support a different and more relevant curriculum.

Another factor here is the way measurement of school performance remains largely tied to measures of student performance within the national curriculum structure. As with access, while the schools by themselves can (and indeed did) make some efforts to match their students' interests more closely, this mismatch between central curriculum and individual need could be tackled much more effectively by groups of schools working together. Such an approach could also take account of local cultural and economic factors that are likely to impact on the future life chances of students. In fact, if access and curriculum content are combined, such that students are offered a broader range of choices across a range of schools, and are able to pursue courses at more than one school, it becomes possible to produce a more balanced and equitable range of opportunities across a local district.

Assessment systems

We have suggested that access and curriculum are issues that might have been tackled in ways that increased educational equity within Stockborough if there had been more substantive collaboration between the schools. However, a further important factor, the way student and school performance is assessed, remains beyond the reach of local districts too. It is an unfortunate fact that government policies in England have promoted extreme levels of competition between schools over recent years, and this has created a climate in which schools look to their own performance first. Consequently, it is understandable that the levels of enthusiasm for networking that we found when the school inquiry teams came together were not reflected in the development of substantive collaborative arrangements between schools. However, even if the schools had developed ways to work together to reduce inequities arising from school access and curriculum, the barriers to equitable schooling posed by the assessment system remain a national, rather than a local district problem.

The current approach to assessment is designed as much as an accountability system for schools as it is a testing regime that can celebrate student achievement or offer a solid basis for determining what students should do next. As such, it has encouraged schools to focus on subjects that will be examined, and students whose interests and aptitude suggest they will succeed in those examinations. Indeed, one could argue that the consequences of the national assessment regime were one of the major reasons that there were groups of marginalised students in these schools to begin with. The assessment system, then, seems to be both a major factor in prompting these schools to address educational equity and a major barrier to the development of truly equitable practices.

Conclusion

As we have seen, within the English policy context equity is rather elusive. Perhaps this is why there was so much discussion during the first year of the SERN project – both within schools and across schools – about what educational equity actually involves, how it is different from equal opportunities strategies, how it can be identified in practice, and whether it can be measured. Indeed, it was discussion about these issues that led the initial group of schools to work on the development of the equity indicators.

At that time there seemed to be a feeling that it should be possible to pin down a definition of equitable schooling, to represent this as a series of dimensions or elements of school processes, and to use these to design an instrument which schools might use to assess the extent to which their own activities were equitable. While the desire to pin down the concept – or better still, develop a single concept of equity that is shared across the participating schools – was both understandable and entirely appropriate, one might ask, with the benefit of hindsight, how far the value of such an instrument was likely to extend beyond those who produced it?

Of course, it could be argued that other schools coming into the network may have been induced to consider the degree of equity in their own provision through the use of such an instrument, which is in itself beneficial. However, it was striking that despite the amount of time and energy put into the development of the instrument by the initial group of schools, new schools drawn into the project actually showed little interest in using it. Our feeling was that this was not because it was a 'poor' instrument but rather because the schools that joined later felt no ownership. It seems that the schools preferred to approach equity on their own terms, exploring it through the experience of their own students. Perhaps it was this same cautious preoccupation with their own situations that led to relatively little real networking for equity across the schools, despite the important developments that took place within the schools.

The analysis of impact we have presented in this chapter points to a paradox that is hugely important for the development of more equitable systems. In the end, equity must be indivisible: either it is everywhere or there is no equity. Yet schools, albeit for understandable reasons, are generally interested in preferring to work outwards from where they are. We might ask whether creating more equitable schooling is amenable to such a partial and segmented approach, or whether we need from the outset to be thinking more widely than the single group of students, the single class, or even the single school. The problem here is that, whilst the way we can identify inequities in the system is by focusing on the present and the particular, the way to tackle them that offers best hope of sustained improvement often requires a wider engagement with those system factors which underlie local inequities, a theme that we explore in the next chapter.

7 Drawing out the lessons

In previous chapters we have seen how schools can investigate their own practices and, in so doing, begin to develop more equitable arrangements. We have
also examined the impact of such activities. The process we have described
involves professionals within a school looking carefully and critically at the
impact of their practices on students. The process, as we have seen, is considerably enhanced if they engage directly with students, as the immediate ben-
eficiaries (or otherwise) of their actions, and if they are supported by critical
friendships with external researchers. It also helps if they are able to engage
with colleagues in other schools who are willing to share experiences, pose
questions and suggest alternative approaches.

Powerful as this approach can be, however, it has significant limitations.
Despite the support and critical friendship that is available from beyond the
school, the focus of individual schools' inquiries almost invariably remains
fixed on what happens within the school. To a significant extent, this is a feature of the inquiry development model itself. Recruiting schools to the project
depended on persuading the head teachers – who controlled the funding that
made the project possible – that there were likely to be clear institutional benefits stemming from systematic inquiry and reflections by staff members on their
own practices. To all intents and purposes, therefore, the heads were signing up
to a school improvement process, albeit one with an explicit concern for equity
issues. The underlying assumption, of course, was that equity issues arise and
can therefore be addressed at the level of the individual school. In this chapter,
we look at why this assumption proved to be somewhat limited in practice. This
leads us to draw out the lessons from the Stockborough experience.

The school as the unit of analysis

As we have explained, following their recruitment, heads were asked to form
cross-hierarchical teams of teachers and other school staff to carry forward the

work. Not surprisingly, these teams focused on what they knew best and what lay most obviously within their control – their own practices in classrooms and, beyond that, the organisational practices of the school as a whole. By and large, teachers and support staff are not required to engage with issues beyond the school, and even if they identify such issues, there is often little they can do to impact upon them. In any case, the sustainability of improvement projects depends on those involved becoming convinced that there is something tangible they can do to enhance educational quality, and therefore, as their critical friends, we were quite happy to encourage them to focus on within-school issues. The situation was doubtless compounded by the fact that head teachers themselves, as the people best placed to look beyond the school gates, were rarely involved in the detailed work of the inquiry teams.

The problem with this essentially inward-looking approach is that what happens *within* schools is inextricably bound up with what happens *between* and *beyond* schools. If equity issues arise around how individual schools treat their students, they also arise around which schools students can access from where they live, who else attends those schools and forms the student's peer group, what educational resources students bring with them from their family and community backgrounds, and what opportunities they have to convert their school experiences into longer-term life chances. None of these things, of course, is directly in the control of the individual school, yet all have a major bearing on how equitable students' educational experiences and opportunities prove to be.

In this situation, there is a real danger that focusing attention on achieving equity within schools' internal practices will overlook important inequities whose origins and impact lie beyond the school. By the same token, there is a parallel danger that the efforts of schools to become more equitable will be overwhelmed by factors from beyond their gates over which they have no control. To an extent, this was the case for some of the schools in SERN.

In order to understand how this happens, we will look more closely at the fate that befell one of the participating schools – Moorside High. In carrying out this analysis, we draw on our interviews with some of those who were closely involved, plus archive material that is mostly in the public domain (e.g. newspaper reports; school performance data; inspection reports). In order to protect the identities of those involved, we have chosen not to provide actual references for these sources.

Our analysis reveals the complexity of those factors that impinged on the educational experiences of students who attended the school and, indeed, on the efforts of school staff to engender positive outcomes. It leads to a story that, in our experience, is not uncommon in schools that serve the most disadvantaged communities – schools that seem to have the odds stacked against them.

A school against the odds

The local environment

Moorside was situated on the outskirts of the main town in Stockborough, about three miles north of its centre, in the middle of a large housing estate that sprawls out across the slopes of adjacent moorland. About 95 per cent of students walked to school, either from this estate or from another equally large estate situated in the neighbouring valley.

The two housing estates are comprised mainly of social housing, built between the 1930s and 1960s, which varies from semi-detached and terraced houses, to flats in high-rise blocks. Many of the original tenants moved here as a result of town centre slum clearances. Later, throughout the sixties and seventies, many more families arrived, some because of the so-called 'white flight' from the town centre, where increasing numbers of Asian families were settling, but also many because of the continuing migration from poor housing in the town.

The local area is characterised by high concentrations of deprivation. Indeed, the communities on the two housing estates are some of the most socially and economically disadvantaged in England, with high levels of youth-offending, teenage pregnancies, and drugs related activity, as well as significant numbers of single-parent families. Crime rates are the highest in Stockborough, with burglary, car crime, arson and crimes of violence commonplace, and with a significant number of the offenders living in the area. Meanwhile, life expectancy for both men and women is seven years less than in neighbouring areas. Employment opportunities for school leavers are limited and those jobs that do exist are mainly in social housing maintenance. In terms of ethnicity, nearly all of the local people are white British and the one (extreme right-wing) British National Party councillor in Stockborough is elected from this area.

Not surprisingly, the student population of Moorside reflected the make-up of these disadvantaged communities. When SERN was established, in 2006, it was a mixed community comprehensive school for 11- to 18-year-olds and had 531 students on roll. Student numbers were declining, and the school was significantly undersubscribed. During that year, 36 per cent of students were eligible for free school meals (the national average was 14 per cent) and 27 per cent of students were on the Special Education Needs register. A significant number of students entered the school with literacy levels well below average.

Social and educational divisions

Among the factors influential in shaping what happened to young people in the district was the make-up of the local secondary school system. As we explained in earlier chapters, the perceived ranking of schools in Stockborough was intensely hierarchical, with Moorside the lowest-status school in the area, taking in for the most part children unable to gain admission to more popular schools in the area.

The nature of this hierarchy deserves more detailed attention. Until 2009, there were sixteen state secondary schools in the area, all accepting both boys and girls. Two of these were selective grammar schools, two were faith schools, and another was a special school for young people defined as having complex learning difficulties. The remaining eleven, all nominally comprehensive schools, were nevertheless hierarchically arranged according to a series of other factors. First of all, six of them were foundation schools – a phenomenon that had its origins in the formation of the local education authority in 1974 from two predecessor boroughs that had selective systems. Some former grammar schools sought to preserve their status by becoming grant-maintained schools (a national policy that allowed schools to opt out of local authority control), and only returned to (limited) local authority control as 'foundation schools' under the Labour government's repatriation scheme in 1997. One consequence of this was that relationships between schools and the local authority were poor, and local authority officers often felt powerless to intervene in school policies. Indeed, we were told that, sometimes, particular officers had not even been able to gain entry to these schools.

Second, the Stockborough schools served communities with very different social characteristics. Some served areas of poor urban housing; others served more affluent semi-rural areas, often preferred by middle-class commuters working in nearby major cities. Inevitably, attainment levels in these two groups of schools tended to reflect the populations they served.

To complicate matters further, the Stockborough area and the schools within it were divided according to student ethnicity. There was a substantial population of families of Pakistani-origin throughout the district, but mainly concentrated in an area of poor housing close to the town centre. The schools serving this area therefore had almost exclusively Pakistani-origin student populations, other schools had substantial Asian heritage minorities, while others were largely white British.

There were, in addition, divisions arising from the structure of post-16 provision locally. Two of the schools serving the most deprived areas did not have any provision for 16- to 18-year-olds. These students had to transfer to other schools, or attend a local college that did not have a very good reputation in the community. Most of the schools that had sixth forms lost some of their post-16 students, either to one or other of the grammar schools, or to a highly regarded sixth form college in a neighbouring local authority.

All of these factors militated against cooperation between the Stockborough secondary schools. This, in turn, reinforced a perception that the schools served different populations, and underlined the different status levels accorded to schools in the local hierarchy. From the point of view of the students, this inevitably meant that their experiences of schooling were coloured to an extent by the reputations their schools enjoyed. Some were able to access well-regarded schools, where levels of academic attainment were high. Others were not selected by these schools, or could not access them because they were too distant from their homes (transport links were often not direct because of the difficult terrain of the area); or had parents who were reluctant to send them to a particular school because of its ethnic mix; or simply had families who were not able or not interested in exercising choice over school placement.

In a bottom-of-the hierarchy school, such as Moorside, the impact of these external factors were striking. In 2006, when we first became involved with the school, attendance at the school was just 82 per cent, one of the lowest in England, as were the school's results in GCSE examinations. In addition, there was a significant number of transient students, who joined the school after Year 7, or left before Year 11. Some families in the local area – particularly the small number of minority ethnic families – chose to send their children to higher-status schools elsewhere. The nearest three high schools were a grammar school and the two faith schools. The next nearest was Central High, just less than two miles to the south, where some 90 per cent of the students were of Asian heritage. Even if students from the two estates wanted to go to one of these other schools and could gain admission, they were relatively difficult to get to by bus.

A troubled past

Given its unpromising social and geographical situation, it is scarcely surprising that Moorside had a troubled history. This history offers an interesting insight into the impact of national efforts to bring about improvements in schools in challenging contexts, particularly the ways the monitoring of performance in the national GCSE examinations and the Ofsted inspection procedures together shape the actions of those involved.

The school had opened in 1995, following what was described as the 'painful merger' of two secondary modern schools – one on the current site, the other a mile and half away – because of declining student numbers. Families had been moving out of the area because of limited employment opportunities, and many of those remaining had been choosing to send their children to other schools with better examination results. Previously, school leavers had found it relatively easy to find low-skilled employment locally, and academic success had not been seen as important.

Within a month of the new school opening, divisions and resentments based on previous school allegiances were already evident. There was also friction between school leaders, governors and the local councillors, not least because students excluded by the school had to be taken back at the insistence of the local authority. The amalgamation had, it seems, brought together 'tribal rivalries' that existed on the local housing estates, leading to poor behaviour, in-school truanting from lessons, and widespread bullying. Overall behaviour in the school was further undermined by a local authority scheme for disaffected students, run in the main teaching block. These students felt they could ignore school rules.

One year later, discipline had further deteriorated, leading to arguments among staff as to what actions should be taken. It was anticipated that there would be an Ofsted inspection, and there was an expectation amongst the staff that the school would fail. Disruption by students continued to escalate, and when a particular student, excluded the term before, was reinstated (having been excluded and reinstated previously) the school made the local newspaper under the headline 'School from hell'. A group of teachers responded by holding a meeting with the national representative from their union. They claimed that as many as sixty students were 'unteachable' and threatened that unless these students were excluded, they would take strike action. Moorside rapidly became the centre of both local and national media attention, with reporters and photographers virtually camping outside the school for the next month.

The head was informed that the school would be given an emergency Ofsted inspection. By the time the inspectors arrived, the front of the school was surrounded by representatives of the national media. The students became increasingly uncontrollable and at lunchtime came out to be interviewed, filmed and photographed. The inspectors informed the head that they thought the school was 'getting out of control'.

The media vigil continued, and footage of students throwing books and a chair were broadcast on the national news. The media coverage culminated in an infamous picture of two girls walking up the school steps behind the head teacher making a 'V' sign. Staff called a lunchtime union meeting and refused to teach timetabled lessons. As a consequence, it was ruled that the school should be closed for a few days, and the head teacher resigned. It was announced that a new person would be taking over as acting head, supported by an associate head from another local school.

The report from the emergency inspection made depressing reading. Only 8 per cent of students achieved five A*–C GCSEs, and 40 per cent did not achieve any qualifications at all. Average attendance was 73 per cent and internal truancy was high. The inspectors required that immediate action be taken '*to restore control and to ensure the physical safety of the students*', and to set up a system whereby the school '*knew the whereabouts of its students*'. Immediate actions were required for improving attainment, the quality of teaching, leadership and management, governors' decision-making, attendance and behaviour, SEN provision, and collaboration between staff members. Unsurprisingly, the school was placed immediately into Special Measures.

Whole school improvement initiatives were launched, monitored closely by Ofsted inspectors, while the two new head teachers immediately excluded some thirty students. Inspectors visited three times between November and December 1996, and then nine times between January 1997 and July 1998. The school then had another full inspection in the autumn of 1998 and was taken out of Special Measures, an occasion that was celebrated as a 'success' for the monitoring regime by both the media and the government. Meanwhile, however, the proportion of students achieving five or more A*–C grades in the GCSE examinations had fallen to 6 per cent in 1997, and then further to only 3 per cent in 1998. Interestingly, these particular statistics were not recorded in the 1998 Ofsted report, although the attendance of 80 per cent was. One of the two heads left in 1997, leaving the other one in charge.

During the next few years, Moorside's apparent progress led to several high-profile visits from ministers, culminating in a visit from the Prime Minister during a national election campaign. Over this period the school received over £6 million to improve its buildings, staffing and resources. There was also a huge turnover of staff and a slight improvement in examination results. In 2001 the school had another full inspection, when it was described as 'a good and improving school', despite attendance still being only 82 per cent. Once again, no examination scores were recorded in this inspection report, despite the fact that in the previous year the Secretary of State had announced that schools failing to get 15 per cent or above in GCSE results for three consecutive years would be closed. For what we assume to have been reasons of political expediency, this did not happen to Moorside.

Subsequently, the school was part of a government-sponsored project aimed at improving schools in challenging circumstances. Despite this intervention GCSE results failed to improve to any great degree and the remaining head teacher resigned in 2005, to be replaced by a head with considerable experience of leading challenging schools. He remained in post until the school was closed in 2009.

The endgame

Four days into his first term, the new head teacher reported to the local authority that, in his opinion, the school should have been placed back into Special Measures. His analysis was that problems in the school ran far deeper than had been publicly admitted, and that these issues had been 'swept under the carpet'. He identified a number of areas of particular concern, such as the high levels of internal truancy. Many of the Year 11 students were, in effect, 'attending part-time' and providing poor role models for the younger students, and student disaffection was 'entrenched'. He was, however, conscious that people from the surrounding neighbourhood were still loyal to the school, and that the local community were well represented among the school governors.

According to the new head's assessment, the quality of teaching was poor, even though the ratio of staff to students was relatively favourable. He also saw that teacher unions were very active in the school, and that there were tensions in the staffroom between well-established and newer members of staff. Another observation was that while many of the teachers who had worked hard to improve the school had moved on, those who had been involved in the 1996 problems had remained in post. It seemed to him that often these staff clashed with newer teachers joining the school. The head's assessment was that '*older staff believed in the students enjoying school but not being successful, whereas the younger staff were more concerned with the students learning and achieving*'. Despite the large financial investment, the new head had found many of the buildings to be in an unsafe state. There was also a budget deficit, making it very hard to appoint new staff.

Soon after his arrival, the school was inspected yet again and judged to be 'inadequate'. Spurred on by this event – which largely confirmed his own assessment of the situation – the new head set out to introduce substantial changes. In effect he divided the school into two, with separate areas of the building for younger and older students, and different uniforms for the two groups. He also introduced a strict discipline strategy, and set up learning support units for students with behavioural, social and emotional difficulties. These started and finished at different times of the day to the mainstream school, and had a different timetable and curriculum.

However, none of this was easily achieved. As new policies were introduced, staff relationships deteriorated further and divisions became even more pronounced. Then in January 2007, as a result of a monitoring visit by inspectors, the school was once again placed in Special Measures, the verdict being that a majority of students were 'underperforming'. The inspectors' report identified the substantial turnover of teachers, failure from some staff to support improvement strategies and long-standing, internal disputes as key reasons for the lack of progress. There were also positive comments, however, including mention of some good lessons, the varied opportunities for sports, support systems for vulnerable students and links with primary schools. It was noted, too, that most students now felt safe at the school. However, students were reported to be anxious about the way their school was reported '*negatively, selec-*

tively and unfairly' in the local and national press, and how this affected their self-esteem.

In the period that followed, local authority staff carried out a review of educational provision in that part of the borough. Eventually, it was decided that Moorside should be closed, since numbers were continuing to fall and there were enough places available in other Stockborough schools to absorb its students. The plan was that, after a break of a year or so, a new academy would be created two miles away, on the site of the two faith schools.

In the meantime, the Moorside staff continued to bring about improvements in teaching and learning, student support, the curriculum and also in the way the school was managed. Ironically, all of this became easier because of the rapidly declining student population. The school's involvement in SERN during this period contributed to these improvements, supporting staff involved in improving teaching and learning across the school. These efforts led to a significant rise in student attendance and noticeable improvements in behaviour during lessons. They were also important from the head's point of view, in that they provided opportunities for improvements to be led from within the school during a period when so much was being determined externally.

As a result, in the summer of 2008, 64 per cent of students achieved five A*–C grades, or equivalent – albeit with a much smaller year group. During the same period, Moorside also came out of Special Measures as a result of 'substantial improvements' in all aspects of its work. Despite these improvements, the decision that the school should close in July 2009 was confirmed, and some staff left as opportunities came up elsewhere. Meanwhile, the local authority nominated an officer to help the transition of students to new schools. For some this was a positive process but for many it was not. Worried by the lack of progress, the head teacher resorted to his own measures, visiting other schools, in some instances virtually having to plead with his colleague head teachers to take his students.

Many of the students moved to Highlands, a school also facing challenging circumstances and dubbed by some as the 'new Moorside'. The remaining students were strongly encouraged to apply for Our Lady's or South Dale, because of the negative experiences of students who had transferred to Highlands during the previous year.

In the final term there were only sixteen students left. By this time, all but one of the secondary schools taking in Moorside students had done so early, in order to enable them to settle in before the summer holidays. Unfortunately this opportunity had not been offered to this small group of students. Many of those who were able to move experienced difficulties settling into their new schools, and in several cases the students changed schools again after only a couple of months. Many of these students combined a history of unusual and unsettled experiences of schooling with a disadvantaged home life, as well as a reputation of coming from a 'bad' school to live down.

Limits of within-school approaches

The SERN project was based on the assumption that schools can have a signifi-cant impact on the nature of their students' educational experiences simply by examining and developing their own practices. Yet this account of Moorside's demise suggests both that what happened to students there was fundamentally unfair and that the origin of this unfairness lay in factors beyond the school's control. While the SERN project was able to support both teachers and stu-dents through a very difficult time, and certainly did promote improvements in the experiences of students within the school, it could do little to address the origins of inequities that reside in a community disadvantaged in so many ways.

As we have explained, the students at Moorside embarked on their second-ary education with significant disadvantages. Some of these were educational, low prior attainment levels, especially in literacy. It seems that something was wrong in their primary schools or, quite probably, that their primary schools were also facing challenges derived from the social and economic disadvan-tages these children suffered and were unable to overcome. These challenges also faced Moorside itself, in terms of deprivation in the areas it served, and the social problems that characterised those areas. Given what we know about the relationship between social disadvantage and educational attainment, it is not surprising that the problems of the area were reflected in low levels of educa-tional attainment among the local population. Moreover, given what we know about the transmission of low achievement through families, it is unsurprising that achievement amongst the children living on the two estates was also low. Writing in *The Guardian* newspaper (3rd May 2011) about life on such estates, Lynsey Hanley commented:

> If you live and are educated in such an area, you may as well live in a penal colony for all that it connects you with a world in which good-quality work, self-confidence and cultural capital – that quality through which the middle classes perpetuate social and economic dominance – are a given.

Despite such circumstances, at various points in its history – particularly towards the end of its life – the Moorside staff were able to have some positive impacts on the attainments of their students. Perhaps it was also the case that the school was an important resource for at least some of its community. At its closure one member of staff who had been at the school since it opened was reported as saying, '*There is a huge need for a small community school there, and I fear that the most vulnerable could now get lost*'.

Undoubtedly, too, the school's participation in SERN played a part in offsetting some of the disadvantages these students faced. However, at no point was Moorside able to fully compensate for the disadvantages its students brought with them into school. Even the improved performance data from its final year disguise the fact that the proportion of students achieving 'C' grades in English and Maths GCSEs remained stubbornly low and, using this measure, the school remained anchored to the foot of the local performance table.

This failure to achieve comparable outcomes from schooling was accompanied by a more limited range of educational experiences during schooling. Indeed, often the reduction in range of experiences is a deliberate strategy adopted in an attempt to increase outcomes; thus the pursuit of one dimension of equity inhibits another. It is not unreasonable to suppose that in schools in one of the wealthiest countries of the world all young people should enjoy a diverse peer group, a relatively stable and committed teaching staff, quality teaching, and a secure school environment throughout their secondary years. None of these were available to the Moorside students. As is so often the case in areas of social disadvantage, they went to school with students like themselves, living in the same area, with similarly low levels of expectation and attainment, and from families with similarly curtailed social and educational experiences. Their teachers came and went with alarming frequency, and in some cases seemed to have preoccupations that had little to do with enabling students to learn. Head teachers, too, appear in some cases to have been concerned with shoring up the school's damaged reputation, whether or not this enhanced the reality of students' experiences or met their educational needs. In such circumstances, it is not surprising that the quality of teaching and organisation was so poor that it attracted the attention of Ofsted. Nor is it surprising that the denouement was closure of the school – though this closure and, particularly, the phased transfer of students to other schools – denied students the stable educational provision that they had a right to expect.

Those school staff members who took part in the SERN project were acutely aware of the structural inequities that hampered their students' progress. However, they could address none of them directly in that work, for the simple reason that they had origins beyond the school, and cannot be altogether offset, even by the improved within-school practices that the SERN project brought about. While both the destructive impact of micro-politics in the staffroom (fed by the unhelpful stance of teacher unions) and the wider policy imperatives driving local and national decision-makers to focus their attention on 'failing' schools without regard for the social contexts of those schools were, to some degree, overcome the struggle was an unequal one. It is not difficult to list the factors that were impediments here, the deprivation scarring the local community, the hierarchical nature of the local school system and the determinants of access, Moorside's position at the bottom of that hierarchy, and the history of 'quick fixes' that had over time denuded the school of many of its most able teachers as it lost its moral compass. In such circumstances, the relatively smooth closure and transfer of students were in themselves important achievements that speak to the commitment of the dwindling band of teachers who remained to the end.

Writing in a letter to a national newspaper in 2008, a member of the local community who had been closely involved in what happened at Moorside offered the following analysis of what had led to the demise of the school:

> It was obvious at the outset that the situation at (Moorside) was the inescapable outcome of an exhaustive selection process. By 1996 pupils in (Stockborough) did not just sit an exam for a grammar school and having failed then attend the local school, they would then join the scramble for places at the highest-regarded available school. This ranking quickly became a widely recognised pecking order, with (Moorside) at the bottom.
>
> From 1997 the school was regularly visited by Labour ministers, who announced success amid orchestrated applause from the media. The rescue myth received the ultimate reinforcement when Tony Blair visited it during the 2001 election campaign to proclaim total victory in the war at (Moorside).
>
> Why was the public so shockingly misled? It seems reasonable to suppose that a covert agenda was in train to implement a policy which not only accepted selection, but greatly extended it – because that is what has happened. Specialist schools, beacon schools and academies, added to grammar schools and church schools, have introduced a multi-layered state system where social class rules and where, inevitably, the devil takes the hindmost.

The writer went on to argue that the north of the town was:

> a well-balanced community with a mix of private and public housing; without the 'creaming-off' inherent in the system, it would have no problem maintaining a full-range-of-ability school, To make (Moorside) viable in 1996 one or, preferably, both of the grammar schools should have been closed. This would have stopped the structural warp and allowed this and other community schools to flourish. Schools would then be equalised, and wasteful and expensive competition between them would reduce.

He concluded the government's approach was leading to a situation where:

> within every education authority the school pushed to the bottom will eventually close, to be replaced by another which will eventually close, ad infinitum. It really is time New Labour stopped scapegoating the poor.

A year after Moorside closed its gates for the last time a new academy opened on the site of the former Long Road High school, with a sponsoring group consisting of a church organisation, a university, the local authority and an educational consultancy company. As the school's admissions policy no longer requires church membership, its catchment area has widened and includes students who would have previously attended Moorside. Nevertheless, a larger number of young people from the two estates continue to travel across the town to Highlands, a school that is itself increasingly working against the odds.

Wider implications

Moorside was an extreme example of how social, economic and educational factors can combine with devastating effects. However, similar factors are at work in other schools involved in the SERN project, though the resulting cocktail is less potent and the impact on schools less dramatic. Nevertheless, we worry about the future prospects for Highlands. In an area where schools are sharply and hierarchically differentiated, the closure of the weakest means that another school finds itself at the bottom of everyone's list.

Highlands is also located on a social housing estate characterised by high levels of deprivation and the associated social and educational problems. However, the estate is a small one, with insufficient school-age children to fill the available places. As a result, Highlands must recruit its students where it can. This is no easy task. Historically, the attainment levels of its students have been low and the school's reputation has been poor. A major rebranding exercise in 2003, with a new school name, uniform, timetable, organisation structure, allegedly new ethos and culture and a new, 'state-of-the-art', environmentally friendly building did provide a boost to recruitment and image. However, the insidious hierarchy among Stockborough schools persists, and Highlands remains at risk.

Several consequences of this vulnerability were visible in Highlands throughout the period of the SERN project. First, the overall size of its student population was on the margins of sustainability, and the bulk of students were children from white working-class families with histories of low educational attainment and the usual range of social and educational problems. In fact, many of the students came from the two estates served by Moorlands, and were effectively fleeing the troubles of that school. Second, the school had little option other than to accept a disproportionately high number of students with poor disciplinary records who were excluded or at risk of exclusion from other schools. These students, of course, frequently brought with them the problems that had made them unwelcome elsewhere. Third, the school also had to accept a disproportionate number of students from recent immigrant families, who did not have English as a first language. A further consequence was that its students were drawn from some twenty-four feeder primary schools, scattered right across the local authority area, and a third of students had joined the school other than in Year 7. To compound its problems, as Moorside began the closure process, Highlands was obliged to accept many of its students, further destabilising its already unstable population.

The manifestations of these external difficulties inside the school were predictable. Attendance remained stubbornly low, at between 80 and 90 per cent, and attainments failed to rise above the government's then floor target of 30 per cent of students attaining five A*–C grades at GCSE. Regular changes of head teacher (there were five during the period of the SERN project!), tensions within the staffroom and conflict between students from new immigrant and long-established families did little to alleviate this situation, and the local authority, with central government encouragement, began looking at what it described as a 'structural solution'. Initial proposals to turn the school into a faith school fell through, and ultimately Highlands was federated with another SERN school, South Dale High. A range of apparently successful organisational practices were imported from the latter into the former, but there was no intention to integrate either the teaching staff or the student populations. As a result, Highlands effectively became a franchise operation for the South Dale 'model', but without any demonstrated improvements in student experiences or outcomes.

Different but related stories could be told about most of the SERN schools. For instance, while the ethnic divides in the area gave Moorside and Highlands overwhelmingly white British populations, they gave Central High a population that was overwhelmingly of Asian heritage. In many ways, students in that school got a good deal, at least to the extent that it managed to fight its way up from the bottom of the local school hierarchy. However, given the political focus on measured attainment as the principal indicator of success, the school achieved this through a combination of 'ability' banding and by giving targeted students high levels of support. The limitations of this approach began to show after the end of statutory schooling, with a worrying proportion of students failing to progress in their post-16 education, where individual support is less readily available.

Indeed, inequities continue to handicap post-16 students in Stockborough's mixed approach to post-16 provision. Central High is another of the schools without a sixth form, meaning that its students too have to transfer to another school in the authority which does, or to the local college, or to a college in a neighbouring authority. Having been nurtured in a highly supportive environment, and having been schooled almost exclusively alongside other members of their ethnic group living in the same small area, Central students struggled with these new social and academic demands, and there were relatively high levels of underachievement and drop-out. Although the SERN team at Central recognised this problem and made it the focus of their inquiries, their principal interest was in demonstrating the need for their school to have its own sixth form provision, rather than in exploring ways in which they could work together with other schools to make the system more equitable and improve their students' post-16 experience.

An ecology of equity

One way to think about the complex processes at work in these schools is to see them as linked within an *ecology of equity*. By this we mean that the extent to which students' experiences and outcomes are equitable is not dependent only on the educational practices of their teachers, or even their schools. Instead, it depends on a whole range of interacting processes that reach into the school from outside. These include the demographics of the areas served by schools, the histories and cultures of the populations who send (or fail to send) their children to the school, and the economic realities faced by those populations. Beyond this, they involve the underlying socio-economic processes that make some areas poor and others affluent, and that draw migrant groups into some places rather than others. They are also influenced by the wider politics of the teaching profession, of local authority decision-making, and of national policy-making, and the impacts of schools on one another over issues such as exclusion and parental 'choice'. In addition, they reflect new models of school governance, the ways in which local school hierarchies are established and maintained, and the ways in which school actions are constrained and enabled by their positions in those hierarchies.

It is important to recognise the complexities of interactions between the different elements in this ecology, and their implications for educational equity. As we worked with schools, we found it helpful to think of three interlinked arenas within which equity issues arose. These were:

*   *Within schools.* These are the issues that arise from school and teacher practices, and are easiest to change through the kind of school-based inquiries characteristic of SERN. They include, amongst other things: the ways in which students are taught and engaged with learning; the ways in which teaching groups are organised and the different kinds of opportunities that result from this organisation; the kinds of social relations and personal support that are characteristic of the school; the ways in which the school responds to diversity in terms of attainment, gender, ethnicity and social background; and the kinds of relationships the school builds with families and local communities.

- *Between-schools.* These are issues that arise from the characteristics of the local school system. They include: the ways in which different types of school emerge locally; the ways in which these schools acquire different statuses so that hierarchies emerge in terms of performance and preference; the ways in which schools compete or collaborate; the processes of integration and segregation which concentrate students with similar backgrounds in different schools; the distribution of educational opportunities across schools; and the extent to which students in every school can access similar opportunities.
- *Beyond-schools.* This far-reaching arena includes: the wider policy context within which schools operate; the family processes and resources which shape how children learn and develop; the interests and understandings of the professionals working in schools; and the demographics, economics, cultures and histories of the areas served by schools. Beyond this, it includes the underlying social and economic processes at national and – in many respects – at global levels out of which local conditions arise.

Looked at in this way, it is clear that there was much that the SERN schools could do to tackle within-school issues, that such actions were likely to have profound impacts on student experiences, and perhaps have some influence on inequities arising elsewhere. Given that Moorside worked for the most part with students who came from families with limited social and educational resources, it was important that it customised provision to meet their needs and wanted to understand how to make this provision work most effectively. Similarly, given that Highlands received many new students – often recent immigrants – throughout the year, it was important that it understood their needs and tried to develop ways of integrating them quickly into the school community. However, it was equally clear that the SERN project did not lead to schools tackling between- and beyond- school issues directly. Whether this was because within-school strategies cannot offset wider inequities in the system or the community, or because they do not prioritise such strategies, is debatable. No school strategy could, for example, make the area served by Moorside more affluent, or increase the resources available to students' families, any more than it could create a stable student population for Highlands, or tackle the global processes underlying migration patterns. But perhaps there are issues of access, or of the allocation of students to schools, than might be tackled if schools work together on a common agenda. Indeed, on several occasions, our university group – acting as critical friends to the school inquiry teams – raised these between- and beyond-school issues, and suggested that the schools might achieve more if they were to work collaboratively on at least some of them. However, as in the case of the sixth form issue at Central High, it was difficult for the school teams to set aside their own school priorities, and explore what it might mean to work more purposefully for equity across institutions. They were working in a context where there were strong pressures on them and their colleagues to see institutional advantage as their overriding concern.

Towards an overarching approach

Despite this somewhat gloomy picture, it is not difficult to see the kinds of policies and practices that would have been needed to tackle at least some of the wider issues facing schools. More to the point, as the SERN project progressed there was evidence that some of these policies and practices were indeed beginning to emerge. To be sure, their appearances were rather patchy – in the form of an initiative here and a policy decision there – rather than a sustained and comprehensive approach. Nonetheless, they showed that despite all the negative forces in their particular equity ecology, something better might indeed be possible.

To take some examples, Highland's vulnerability from being required to accept excluded students was reduced significantly partway through the project, when the local authority brokered an agreement between schools to manage exclusions in a way that did not result in the 'dumping' of students on whichever school happened to have spare places. Whilst the agreement was far from perfect, at the very least it indicated that schools might begin to think of themselves collectively as responsible not just for their own populations, but for all children in the area. At the same time, it showed that the local authority might play a key role in representing the wider community interest and enabling competitor institutions to think in terms other than of their own advantage. To a degree, this was paralleled by the creation of the South Dale/Highlands federation. Although the enforced relationship between the two schools was unquestionably problematic, at the same time it indicated that the traditional pattern of individual schools competing against one another was by no means the only one available.

Developments of this kind indicated some ways in which what we have called between-schools issues might have been tackled. However, there were also indications that beyond-school issues were not so far out of reach as they might at first seem. The head at Moorside, for instance, shortly before it closed, talked about what he would have liked to set in place had the school remained open. He argued that the life chances of the young people in his care depended on their finding employment, but that much of the employment in the area was offered not by large companies, but by small – often one-person – enterprises such as hairdressers, sandwich shops and handyman businesses. He wanted, therefore, to locate businesses of this kind on the school site and to integrate work experience with them into the school curriculum. In this way, he felt, the school could contribute directly to the local economy, give students a different – and perhaps more engaging – learning experience, and develop in them skills and knowledge that would transfer more readily into the workplace.

Through a different process, the head teacher at Central High also began to see new possibilities for how schools might operate. For the first part of the project, he was focused almost exclusively on within-school issues and, indeed, on the single task of driving-up his students' measured attainment levels. When asked about wider equity issues, he commented wryly, '*When I took over, this school was very equitable. Everyone failed.*' However, partway through the project he left the school to manage a borough-wide change programme aimed at fostering an integrated approach to working with children and families across local authority services, the health service and the voluntary sector. The programme itself was short-lived and by no means an unqualified success, but its aims were novel in Stockborough – to bring about cultural change in the ways schools and services worked by facilitating collaboration, finding successful examples of collaboration in action, and identifying key professionals who could champion new ways of working. Equally interesting was the ex-head teacher's response. By his own admission, he learnt for the first time how the world of children's services beyond school worked, and the range of agencies and structures that impacted on the lives of his former students. As a result, he became an enthusiast for a more holistic approach to children's development, and freely admitted embarrassment that he had apparently been able to become a successful head teacher without ever having to engage with this wider world.

One of the principal contributions to this change programme came from the work of another Stockborough school, Outwood, which only participated in SERN during the final year. The school was located in a small post-industrial town somewhat remote from the other population centres, but facing similar issues to those besetting Moorside and Highlands. The town had lost its major employer, and local income levels, expectations and attainment levels were low. However, the head teacher took the view that he could not focus simply on the within-school consequences of this situation, but had to tackle some of these problems at source. He therefore set about creating a 'learning community' in the town, initiating or supporting several projects linking the school with other agencies and organisations concerned with regenerating the area, and working with local community groups to facilitate their programmes. Most importantly, he established an inter-professional network in which workers from different agencies were encouraged to build partnerships to take joint actions on problems and possibilities in the town. The model was seen as sufficiently successful for it to be promoted by the authority, and for other schools in the authority to begin to adopt it.

Conditions for fostering equity

Neither the setting up of this inter-professional network, nor any of the other developments we have described above were problem-free. But in the context of the fragmented, hierarchical Stockborough school system, and the over-whelming social problems experienced in some parts of the authority, even piecemeal approaches – heavily dependent on the interests and enthusiasm of individuals who themselves sometimes came and went with great rapidity – are preferable to doing nothing. Maybe the majority of such initiatives are likely to endure only as long as their sponsors and favourable circumstances can be maintained, but some sow seeds that will root and grow. We were also aware that developments in Stockborough could sometimes appear rather pale shadows of equivalent developments that could be found elsewhere in the country, but it seems that when it comes to significant cultural change, every Stockborough needs to develop its own approach.

So, despite these limitations, the experiences we have described in this book indicate what is necessary – in addition to the kind of within-school developments promoted by the SERN project – in order that substantial issues of educational equity can be addressed in a meaningful way at the system-level. In summary, five organisational conditions need to be in place for this to happen:

Condition 1: Schools have to collaborate in ways that create a whole-system approach. If, as we have argued, equity issues can arise between schools, then an approach to promoting equity is needed which crosses school boundaries. Put simply, all schools in an area need to assume some level of account-ability for all of the children who live in that area. As the Stockborough agreement on exclusions illustrates, schools can and should consider how their individual actions impact on other schools and, more particularly, on the children who attend those other schools. This means that the priori-tisation of institutional advantage that is so characteristic of the current school system needs to be replaced by an approach that acknowledges the *mutuality* of schools. Put another way, the unit of analysis in relation to equity needs to be broadened beyond the individual school – and this may, of course, have implications for how and for what schools are held to account.

Condition 2: Equity-focused local leadership is needed in order to coordinate collabora-tive action. Given its troubled history and the fragmentation of the local school system, the Stockborough local authority was, for the most part, in no position to persuade schools to act on the principles of equity rather than of institutional advantage. Whatever the strengths of the individu-als who tried to manage this difficult situation, Stockborough was, in this respect, a weak local authority. Yet we see from the examples above that when it was able to be pro-active and to give a lead to schools, it was able to change the focus of their actions so that they began to consider the wider implications of how they behaved. Whether local authorities are any longer the appropriate vehicles for local coordination and policy-making is a moot point, but it is clear that some source of local leadership is needed, and that such leadership has to be concerned with equity issues across the area rather than with the advantage of this or that institution.

Condition 3: Development in schools must be linked to wider community efforts to tackle inequities experienced by children. Local coordination is not simply about managing schools into some sort of productive relationship with each other. It is also about linking the work of schools with that of other agencies, organisations and community groups that are concerned with the social and economic well-being of the area. Working individually, schools are helpless to tackle the deprivation and associated disadvantages that some of their students experience. Yet, as we have seen, there is no reason in principle why they cannot look beyond their gates and develop more holistic approaches to local problems in collaboration with other stakeholders. The precise role to be played by schools in such approaches remains a matter for debate, but it is schools that have the readiest access to children and families, that are typically located geographically within the communities they serve, that are responsible for educating the parents, workers and citizens of the future, and that have substantial resources in terms of personnel and facilities available to play a part in developing area well-being. Whilst retaining their primary focus on teaching and learning, therefore, it makes sense for schools to be reconceptualised – as some of the Stockborough head teachers were beginning to see – as part of a network of community resources able to make a real difference to local contexts.

Condition 4: National policy has to be formulated in ways that enable and encourage local actions. None of the developments we are suggesting will be possible without a national policy framework that encourages schools to orientate themselves towards wider equity issues. The perverse consequences of successive governments' education policies are all too evident in the Stockborough situation: the narrow focus on measured attainment; the conflation of crude benchmarks of school performance with students' real achievements; the encouragement of schools to view themselves as self-interested institutions competing against each other rather than working in the interests of all children; the weakening of local leadership from local authorities; the repeated attempts to solve deep-seated social and educational problems by improving, reforming and, ultimately, closing down the schools where those problems became manifest. Yet this is not the whole story of education policy over the past two decades. The nascent forms of school collaboration in Stockborough owed much to a policy emphasis on schools working together, and an unheralded yet crucial shift away from the 'lone school' model for providing education. Likewise, the holistic approach to an area's problems is engendered directly by government insistence on integrating child and family services, on developing so-called 'joined-up' approaches to area regeneration, and on 'extending' the role of schools to incorporate work with families and communities. The implication is that, even in what appear to be quite unpromising circumstances, national policy can provide important frameworks within which schools can work with their partners to develop wide-ranging approaches to equity, focusing not just on what happens within the school, but also on what happens between and beyond schools.

Condition 5· Moves to foster equity in education must be mirrored by efforts to develop a fairer society. Needless to say, even the most powerful area-based approaches to promoting equity are likely to have little more than palliative effects in the context of the powerful socio-economic forces that engender inequality and lead to marginalisation. There is, therefore, an important sense in which, in the absence of more fundamental social reforms, the efforts to develop greater equity and service integration in Stockborough are inevitably doomed to failure. Yet, powerful as the forces that produce inequality and marginalisation might be, they are not entirely overwhelming. Policy in this country and elsewhere can and does make a difference to levels of poverty, to social segregation and integration, and to the gaps between rich and poor. Even without radical political change, different governments as a matter of record, have made different decisions that exacerbate or ameliorate the impact of both underlying socio-economic processes and global influences.

Conclusion

We have argued that the SERN process, as described in this book, represents a worthwhile but nevertheless limited response to issues of inequity in schools. To say that it is limited is not to say that it is not worth doing, nor that the efforts of the many teachers whose enthusiasm and commitment drove the project have not already touched many of their students. Even small improvements are worthwhile if they can make educational experiences more equitable and outcomes more positive for some students than they otherwise might have been. Moreover, the SERN process is only 'limited' if it remains an isolated intervention in schools, school systems and societies which are otherwise unchanged.

Our view is that, just as there is a complicated ecology of equity in and around schools, so there needs to be multi-dimensional strategies to tackle equity issues. Specifically, school-based inquiry processes need to be nested within locally led efforts to make school systems more equitable and to link the work of schools with area strategies for tackling wider inequities and, ultimately, with national policies aimed at creating a more equitable society.

The hope that such a coherent, nested approach will appear overnight in England, or indeed anywhere else, may seem in vain. On the other hand, it is by no means to be assumed that everything beyond the school will be hostile to the promotion of equity, and even in the unpromising policy context in which the SERN project took place, there were encouraging developments and indications of how a more coherent approach might take shape. If radical reform is improbable, a more imperfect, longer-term and piecemeal process of change might be the most sensible way to inch towards it.

8 Rethinking the tasks

Our involvement in Stockborough over five years provided us with rich opportunities for learning. In particular, through our partnerships with colleagues in the schools, we found ourselves in a privileged position to learn from them and with them. In so doing, we were able to share in some of their successes, experience some of the difficulties they face on a day-to-day basis, and feel some of their frustrations as they tried to do their best for the students within the particular policy context.

All of this has affirmed our commitment to the overall approach we have explained and illustrated in the earlier chapters. In particular, it has provided convincing evidence that inquiry can be a powerful strategy for fostering equity within schools. It has also deepened our understanding of the sorts of techniques that are required, and how their use has to take account of political and cultural factors within particular school contexts.

The length of our involvement was a significant factor – usually such initiatives are for much shorter periods. In this case it allowed us to track the way improvement efforts developed over time and the way changes in the context influenced what happened. This helped us to appreciate the limitations of the approach we were developing, particularly where it concentrates solely on within-school factors, important though these are. As a result, we have broadened our approach to involve between-school and beyond-school factors. This led us to formulate a series of *organisational conditions* that are, we suggest, necessary in order to move education systems in a more equitable direction. These conditions are:

- Schools have to collaborate in ways that create a whole-system approach.
- Equity-focused local leadership is needed in order to coordinate collaborative action.
- Development in schools must be linked to wider community efforts to tackle inequities experienced by children.

- National policy has to be formulated in in ways that enable and encourage local action.
- Moves to foster equity in education must be mirrored by efforts to develop a fairer society.

Bearing all of this in mind, in this final chapter we consider the implications of our findings. This leads us to make recommendations as to what needs to be done – in our country and elsewhere – in order to develop more equitable education systems. Drawing on what we have learnt in Stockborough, and connecting this to evidence from our work in other places, these recommendations involve an approach based on an analysis of contexts and processes of networking and collaboration in order to make better use of available expertise. This approach has significant implications for all those concerned with educational improvement. Put simply, it requires them to rethink their tasks. It also requires clarity of purpose regarding the idea of equity.

Rethinking equity in education

An OECD report, 'No more failures: ten steps to equity in education' (2007) argues that educational equity has two dimensions. First, it is a matter of *fairness*, which implies ensuring that personal and social circumstances – for example gender, socio-economic status or ethnic origin – should not be an obstacle to achieving educational potential. Second, it is to do with *inclusion*, which is about ensuring a basic minimum standard of education for all. The report notes that the two dimensions are closely intertwined since, *'tackling school failure helps to overcome the effects of social deprivation which often causes school failure'* (p. 11).

The report goes on to argue that a fair and inclusive education is desirable because of the human rights imperative for people to be able to develop their capacities and participate fully in society. It also reminds us of the long-term social and financial costs of educational failure, since those without the skills to participate socially and economically generate higher costs for health, income support, child welfare and security. In addition, increased migration poses new challenges for social cohesion in more and more countries.

Despite the efforts made in response to such arguments, in many parts of the world there remains a worrying gap between the achievements of students from rich and poor families (UNESCO, 2010). The extent of this gap varies significantly between countries. For example, Mourshed, Chijioke and Barber (2010: 8-9) argue:

> In a world-class system like Finland's, socioeconomic standing is far less predictive of student achievement. All things being equal, a low-income student in the United States is far less likely to do well in school than a

low-income student in Finland. Given the enormous economic impact of educational achievement, this is one of the best indicators of equal opportunity in a society.

On a more optimistic note, the most recent international comparisons in relation to literacy indicate that the best performing school systems manage to provide high-quality education for all of their students. For example:

> Canada, Finland, Japan, Korea and the partner economies Hong Kong-China and Shanghai-China all perform well above the OECD mean performance and students tend to perform well regardless of their own background or the school they attend. They not only have large proportions of students performing at the highest levels of reading proficiency, but also relatively few students at the lower proficiency levels.
>
> (OECD, 2010, p. 15)

The implication is that it is possible for countries to develop education systems that are both excellent and equitable. The question is: what needs to be done to move policy and practice forward?

Within the international research community there is evidence of a division of opinion regarding how to respond to this question. On the one hand, there are those who argue that what is required is a school-focused approach, with better implementation of the knowledge base that has been created through many years of school effectiveness and improvement research (e.g. Hopkins *et al.*, 2005; Sammons, 2007). Such researchers point to examples of where this approach has had an impact on the performance of schools serving disadvantaged communities (e.g. Chenoweth, 2007; Stringfield, 1995). On the other hand, there are those who argue that such school-focused approaches can never address fundamental inequalities in societies that make it difficult for some young people to break with the restrictions imposed on them by their home circumstances (Dyson and Raffo, 2007). So, for example, Fryer and Levitt (2004) cite research in the United States that shows how racial and socio-economic achievement gaps are formed before children even enter school, whilst Phillips *et al.* (1998) and Fryer and Levitt (2004) argue that one-third to one-half of the gap can be explained by family-environment factors. And talking about recent reform efforts in the United Kingdom, Ball (2010: 156) argues:

> The overwhelming focus of education policy . . . on "raising standards" has done very little and perhaps can do no more to close performance outcome gaps between social class groups. I am not saying that standards have not been raised (whatever that might mean and whatever value in terms of public good that might deliver) but that performance gaps in terms of social class remains enormous. . . . My point is that if we want to understand and explain persistent educational inequalities and do something

about them through policy, then increasingly, the school is the wrong place to look and the wrong place to reform – at least in isolation from other sorts of changes in other parts of society.

Such arguments point to the danger of separating the challenge of school improvement from a consideration of the impact of wider social and political factors. This danger is referred to by those who recommend more holistic reforms that connect schools, communities and external political and economic institutions (e.g. Anyon, 1997; Crowther *et al.*, 2003; Levin, 2005; Lipman, 2004). These authors conclude that it is insufficient to focus solely on the improvement of individual schools. Rather, such efforts must be part of a larger overarching plan for system-wide reform that must include all stakeholders, at the national, district, institutional and community levels.

An obvious possibility is to combine the two perspectives by adopting strategies that seek to link attempts to change the internal conditions of schools with efforts to improve local areas. This approach is a feature of the highly acclaimed Harlem Children's Zone (Whitehurst and Croft, 2010), a neighbourhood-based system of education and social services for the children of low-income families in New York. The programme combines education components (e.g. early childhood programmes with parenting classes, public charter schools); health components (including nutrition programmes); and neighbourhood services (one-on-one counselling for families, community centres, and a centre that teaches job-related skills to teenagers and adults). Dobbie and Fryer (2009) describe the Children's Zone as 'arguably the most ambitious social experiment to alleviate poverty of our time' (p. 1). Having carried out an in-depth analysis of statistical data regarding the impact of the initiative, they conclude: *'high-quality schools or high-quality schools coupled with community investments generate the achievement gains. Community investments alone cannot explain the results'* (p. 25).

Our recommendations are based on this combined approach, although we are well aware that pressures created by national policies can lead to strategic dilemmas, particularly when schools feel obliged to demonstrate rapid increases in test and examination scores.

Rethinking policy

In thinking about how the strategies we have outlined in this book might be used more widely it is essential to recognise that they do not offer a set of techniques that can simply be lifted and transferred to other contexts. Rather, they offer an overall approach to improvement that is driven by a set of values and uses processes of contextual analysis in order to create strategies that fit particular circumstances. What is also distinctive in the approach is that it is mainly led from within schools in order to make more effective use of existing expertise and creativity.

We have also argued that closing the gap in outcomes between those from more and less advantaged backgrounds will only happen when what happens to children *outside* as well as *inside* schools changes. This means changing how families and communities work, and enriching what they offer to children. In this respect we have seen encouraging experiences elsewhere of what can happen when what schools do is aligned in a coherent strategy with the efforts of other local players – employers, community groups, universities and public services (Ainscow, 2012; Cummings, Dyson and Todd, 2011). This does not necessarily mean schools doing more, but it does imply partnerships beyond the school, where partners multiply the impacts of each other's efforts.

All of this has implications for the various key stakeholders within education systems. In particular teachers, especially those in senior positions, have to see themselves as having a wider responsibility for all children and young people, not just those that attend their own schools. They also have to develop patterns of internal organisation that enable them to have the flexibility to cooperate with other schools and with stakeholders beyond the school gate (Chapman *et al.*, 2008). It means, too, that those who administer area school systems have to adjust their priorities and ways of working in response to improvement efforts that are led from within schools.

There is a key role for governments in all of this. The evidence from the English experience over the last twenty years suggests that attempts to command and control from the centre stifle as many local developments as they stimulate (Ainscow and West, 2006; Gray, 2010; Whitty, 2010). Consequently, central government needs to act as an enabler, encouraging developments, disseminating good practice and holding local leaders to account for outcomes. All of this depends on the currency of knowledge exchange and, therefore, requires cultural change. This requires a new approach to national policy, one that can respond to local factors while also providing a unifying understanding of equity that can help to create coherence and foster collaboration across reform efforts (Ainscow, 2005). In this respect, there is a need for policy that will help to:

- **Achieve a common sense of purpose.** It is vital that educational professionals are guided by some common understanding of equity – not a singular and absolute understanding, but one which is based around a shared framework of values and principles, and can accommodate different responses to diverse local needs. This is central to the development of common understandings regarding the purposes and requirements of proposals for equitable reform.

- **Establish processes of accountability.** The emphasis in many countries on measurable attainments as the central indicator of educational success – and, therefore, of the equitability of the education system – must be rethought. We must develop ways to measure what we truly value in terms of an equity agenda, not just to measure that which can easily be assessed. In so doing, we must move away from reductionist thinking that focuses on a narrow range of educational performances, in order to explore wider outcomes and processes of education in relation to principles of equity.
- **Coordinate local action.** Greater local coordination, as opposed to measures to enhance the autonomy of individual institutions, appears necessary to challenge locally ingrained patterns of inequity. Central to this, the role of local authorities as 'place shapers' must be rethought so that they are appropriately placed and have sufficient powers to coordinate local action in line with an equity agenda.

All of this means that government must engage with the question of how to incorporate 'the local' into national policy. In so doing, the assumption that usually underpins national improvement strategies in many countries – that what is good for one school is good for all schools – must be challenged. Policy-makers must also give serious consideration to the sorts of evidence they need from the system to inform policy developments and how this can be used.

Rethinking the way schools work

At the heart of the approach outlined in this book is the idea of those *within schools* collecting and engaging with various forms of data in order to stimulate moves to create more equitable arrangements. The accounts we have presented provide a convincing case for the power of this approach. In so doing, they offer a vision of schools as places where inquiry is at the heart of everything that goes on. In this way, they become schools that are on the move, always seeking new ways to reach out to all of their students, particularly those that miss out within existing ways of working. As we have argued, this means that they become learning organisations, where – however well they are doing – there is a continuing search for new possibilities for improving their practices.

Our accounts have thrown light on the difficulties in putting such an approach into practice within current policy contexts. This has led us to analyse the limitations of within-school strategies, leading us, in turn, to argue that these should be complemented with between-schools and beyond-schools activities.

In terms of collaboration between schools, our overall assessment of what happened in Stockborough is rather disappointing. Whilst the school teams undoubtedly learnt a great deal from one another, our efforts to encourage more of the sorts of joint inquiry and development activities that we witnessed in the inclusion project described in Chapter 2 were largely ineffective. This is a matter of particular concern since it is clear from our analysis that the unfair treatment of some young people – such as the limitations placed on post-16 opportunities – arose as a result of the dynamics between schools.

In recent years, we have carried out a series of studies that have generated considerable evidence that school-to-school collaboration can strengthen improvement processes by adding to the range of expertise made available (see: Ainscow, 2010; Ainscow, Muijs and West, 2006; Ainscow, Nicolaidou and West, 2003; Ainscow and West, 2006; Ainscow, West and Nicolaidou, 2005; Chapman *et al.*, 2010; Muijs, West and Ainscow, 2010; Muijs, Ainscow, Chapman and West, 2011). Together, these studies indicate that school-to-school collaboration has an enormous potential for fostering system-wide improvement, particularly in challenging urban contexts. More specifically, they show how collaboration between schools can provide an effective means of solving immediate problems, such as staffing shortages, how it can have a positive impact in periods of crisis, such as during the closure of a school and how, in the longer run, schools working together can contribute to the raising of expectations and attainment in schools that have had a record of low achievement. There is also evidence here that collaboration can help to reduce the polarisation of schools according to their position in 'league tables', to the particular benefit of those students who seem marginalised at the edges of the system and whose performance and attitudes cause increasing concern.

For the most part, these studies have focused on situations where schools have been given short-term financial incentives linked to the demonstration of collaborative planning and activity. Nevertheless, they convince us this approach can be a powerful catalyst for change, although it does not represent an easy option, particularly in policy contexts within which competition and choice continue to be the main policy-drivers.

The most convincing evidence about the power of schools working together comes from our recent involvement in the Greater Manchester Challenge. This three-year project, which involved a partnership between national government, ten local authorities and over 1,100 schools, had a government investment of around £50million (see Ainscow, 2012, for a detailed account of this initiative). The decision to invest such a large budget reflected a concern regarding educational standards in the city region, particularly amongst children and young people from disadvantaged backgrounds. The approach adopted was influenced by an earlier initiative in London (Brighouse, 2007)

Reflecting much of the thinking developed in this book, the overall approach of the Challenge emerged from a detailed analysis of the local context, using both statistical data and local intelligence provided by stakeholders. This drew attention to areas of concern and also helped to pinpoint a range of human resources that could be mobilised in order to support improvement efforts. Recognising the potential of these resources, it was decided that networking and collaboration should be the key strategies for strengthening the overall improvement capacity of the system. More specifically this involved a series of interconnected activities for *moving knowledge around*.

So, for example, in an attempt to engage all schools in processes of networking and collaboration, Families of Schools were set up, using a data system that groups between twelve and twenty schools on the basis of the prior attainment of their students and their socio-economic home backgrounds. The strength of this approach is that it partners schools that serve similar populations whilst, at the same time, encouraging partnerships amongst schools that are not in direct competition with one another because they do not serve the same neighbourhoods. Led by head teachers, the Families of Schools proved to be successful in strengthening collaborative processes within the city region, although the impact was varied.

In terms of schools working in highly disadvantaged contexts, evidence from the Challenge suggests that school-to-school partnerships are the most powerful means of fostering improvements. Most notably, the *Keys to Success* programme led to striking improvements in the performance of some 160 schools facing the most challenging circumstances. There is also evidence that the progress that these schools made helped to trigger improvement across the system. A common feature of almost all of these interventions was that progress was achieved through carefully matched pairings (or, sometimes, trios) of schools that cut across social 'boundaries' of various kinds, including those that separate schools that are in different local authorities. In this way, expertise that was previously trapped in particular contexts was made more widely available.

Another effective strategy to facilitate the movement of expertise was provided through the creation of various types of *hub schools*. So, for example, some of the hubs provided support for other schools regarding ways of supporting students with English as an additional language. Similarly, so-called 'teaching schools' providing professional development programmes focused on bringing about improvements in classroom practice. Other hub schools offered support in relation to particular subject areas, and in responding to groups of potentially vulnerable groups, such as those with special educational needs. In this latter context, a further significant development involved new roles for special schools in supporting developments in the mainstream.

Significantly, we found that such arrangements can have a positive impact on the learning of students in all of the participating schools. This is an important finding in that it draws attention to a way of strengthening relatively low performing schools that can, at the same time, help to foster wider improvements in the system. It also offers a convincing argument as to why relatively strong schools should support other schools. Put simply, the evidence is that by helping others you help yourself.

Whilst increased collaboration of this sort is vital as a strategy for developing more effective ways of working, the experience of Greater Manchester showed that it is not enough. The essential additional ingredient is an engagement with data that can bring an element of mutual challenge to such collaborative processes. We found that data were particularly essential when partnering schools, since collaboration is at its most powerful where partner schools are carefully matched and know what they are trying to achieve. Data also matters in order that schools go beyond cosy relationships that have no impact on outcomes. Consequently, schools need to base their relationships on evidence about each other's strengths and weaknesses, so that they can challenge each other to improve.

In order to facilitate this kind of contextual analysis, strategies and frameworks were devised to help schools to support one another in carrying out reviews. In the primary sector, this involved colleagues from another school acting as critical friends to internally driven review processes; whilst in secondary schools, subject departments took part in 'deep dives', where skilled specialists from another school visited in order to observe and analyse practice, and promote focused improvement activities. The power of these approaches is in the way they provide teachers with opportunities to have strategic conversations with colleagues from another school.

The powerful impact of the collaborative strategies developed in the Greater Manchester Challenge points to ways in which the processes used in Stockborough could be deepened and, therefore, strengthened. This would require much more emphasis on mutual critique, within schools and between schools, based on an engagement with shared data. This, in turn, requires strong collective commitment from senior school staff and a willingness to share responsibility for system reform. Our recent study of new patterns of school leadership that are emerging in response to the structural changes occurring in the English education system offer some promise in this respect (Chapman *et al.*, 2008).

Rethinking contexts

Moving to a *beyond-school* focus, our analysis in Chapter 7 of the way external factors limited the possibilities for further developments at Moorside and Highlands schools offers a vivid illustration of the complexities involved. In so doing it makes a convincing case for carrying out an analysis of the wider context within which schools work.

We have had considerable experiences of conducting such analyses in other districts. This has convinced us that transforming educational provision in relation to local neighbourhoods and services depends on identifying local priorities and ways of developing sustainable responses to these. To do this, it is necessary to engage in forms of contextual analysis that probe beneath the surface of headline performance indicators in order to understand how local dynamics shape particular outcomes; identify the key underlying factors at work; and determine which of these factors can be acted upon and by whom.

This marks a shift in thinking about local transformation from a surface-level, quick-fix response – concerned with manipulating headline figures – to a deeper response, which by addressing issues in context aims to achieve sustainable and long-term improvements. In this way, the purpose is to produce a rich and actionable understanding of local issues. To help achieve this, the analysis may be bounded in one of three ways – none of which are mutually exclusive:

- **By the unit of action** – for example, a contextual analysis might focus on issues in an administratively defined area, such as a district or local authority, where there are already structures in place that can be used to drive action.
- **By geographical and social boundaries** – the analysis might focus on issues in an area that has clear physical boundaries, for example, main roads, or imagined boundaries, such as a housing estate that residents strongly identify with – or some combination of the two.
- **By issues** – the analysis might focus on understanding a particular issue, such as poor school attendance or teenage gang membership. In these instances, while retaining a local focus, the analysis might extend beyond a particular neighbourhood or administrative area.

We have found that sometimes a contextual analysis may highlight issues that shape local circumstances but which local actors are not in a position to change – for example, global recession leading to the decline of local industry. However, the analysis should be able to identify how local processes and dynamics are being shaped by this; what is locally actionable; and what unit(s) of action can be utilised to develop an appropriate response.

In order to understand the complex dynamics at work in an area, as well as exploring outcome data, it is necessary to enable people who live and work there to talk about their understandings of local issues. We have found that a loose research framework can help to provide the freedom needed for this, while also ensuring that the data generated can be usefully compared, and used to create shared understandings and strategies. For example, to explore issues

Table 8.1 A framework for area analysis

Aspects of formal education	*Core questions*			
	What is it like round here?	*Why is it like this?*	*Is it a problem?*	*What can be done?*
Getting in *(accessing education)*				
Taking part *(participation and processes)*				
Moving on *(outcomes and destinations)*				

of educational equity in context, we have used frameworks such as the one in Table 8.1 in order to guide data generation.

Similarly, a sampling strategy can be drawn up to ensure that a range of stakeholder views are accessed. A further helpful exercise is to map the existing resources being used to address local issues, and to explore how connections between these can be forged.

Rethinking relationships

Central to the strategies we have described in this book are attempts to develop new, more fruitful working relationships: between national and local government; between administrators and practitioners; within and between schools; and between schools and their local communities. A helpful theoretical interpretation that can be made of these strategies is that, together, they may help to strengthen *social capital*. In other words, they can establish pathways through which energy, expertise and lessons from innovations can spread.

In recent years, the work of Robert Putnam (2000) has been most influential in making the idea of social capital a focus for research and policy discussion. In so doing, he has demonstrated how it can help to mitigate the insidious effects of socio-economic disadvantage. Writing about the United States, for example, Putnam states that '*what many high-achieving school districts have in abundance is social capital, which is educationally more important than financial capital*' (p. 306). Reflecting on his work with schools serving disadvantaged communities – also in the United States – Payne (2008: 39) comes to a similar conclusion. Thinking specifically about schools contexts that are characterised by low levels of social capital, he argues:

> Weak social infrastructure means that conservatives are right when they say that financial resources are likely to mean little in such environments. It means that expertise inside the building is likely to be underutilized, and

expertise coming from outside is likely to be rejected on its face. It means that well-thought-out programs can be undermined by the factionalized character of teacher life or by strong norms that militate against teacher collaboration.

This leads him to conclude that such schools are unlikely to learn from their experience since 'it is difficult to learn from people one does not respect'.

Focusing more specifically on schools, Mulford (2007) defines social capital in terms of the groups, networks, norms and trust that people have available to them for productive purposes. He goes on to suggest that by treating social relationships as a form of capital, they can be seen as a resource, which people can then draw on to achieve their goals. There are, he explains, three types of social capital, each of which throws further light on the processes that could be developed within an education system. The first of these is 'bonding social capital' – this relates to what can happen amongst work colleagues within a school. 'Bridging social capital' is what can occur between schools through various forms of networking and collaboration. And finally, 'linking social capital' relates to stronger relationships between a school and wider community resources.

The recommendations we are making suggest a series of interconnected strategies that may help to foster stronger social capital of all three types. These strategies can help to break down social barriers within schools, between schools, and between schools and other stakeholders, in order to facilitate the sorts of mutual benefit that we have described. In this sense, the strategies provide the basis for what Hargreaves (2010) describes as a 'self-improving school system'. In terms of our developing argument, this means moving away from the idea of individual schools as learning organisations, to the development of school systems that have a greater capacity for learning and development.

Having said that, we must be wary at this point of falling into the trap of suggesting that all of this is simple and straightforward. For example, writing about the idea of school networks as an improvement strategy, Lima (2008: 2) argues:

> Despite their growing prevalence, networks have become popular mainly because of faith and fads, rather than solid evidence on their benefits or rigorous analyses of their characteristics, substance and form . . . there is nothing inherently positive or negative about a network: it can be flexible and organic, or rigid and bureaucratic; it can be liberating and empowering, or stifling and inhibiting; it can be democratic, but it may also be dominated by particular interests.

It is also important to recognise that the gains made through such approaches are likely to be hard won, and may therefore remain fragile and easily lost.

Here, continuing tensions regarding priorities and preferred ways of working between national and local policy-makers, and, indeed, between schools and local authorities, remain factors that can continue to create barriers to progress. So, for example, those near to central government may remain preoccupied with achieving short-term gains in test and examination scores in ways that can create barriers to efforts for promoting sustainable improvements. Coupled with this may be a mistrust of local authorities – the staff of which are sometimes seen as part of the problem, rather than part of the solution – and doubts about the need to have separate strategies that fit particular contexts.

Rethinking local coordination

The creation of education systems where improvement is driven by schools themselves, and that involves cooperation between schools, and between schools and other community organisations, begs questions regarding the roles of local authorities. Indeed, it raises the possibility that the involvement of a middle-level administrative structure may not even be necessary.

The authors of the influential McKinsey report, having analysed 'how the world's most improved school systems keep getting better', express their surprise at the critical role that what they call the 'mediating layer' plays between school delivery and central government (Mourshed, Chijioke and Barber, 2010). This leads them to conclude that sustaining system improvement in the longer term requires 'integration and intermediation' across each level of the system, 'from the classroom to the superintendent or minister's office'. They explain:

> The operating system of the mediating layer acts as the integrator and mediator between the classrooms and the centre. This is not to suggest that school reforms should begin here. In every system we looked at, the first focus of school reforms was on the schools and the centre. Efforts to strengthen the mediating layer usually came later, as the need for an active intermediary in delivering the system improvements became clearer.
>
> (Mourshed, Chijioke and Barber, 2010: 82)

The authors of the report go on to suggest that the specific functions the mediating layer plays are: providing targeted support to schools; acting as a buffer between the centre and the schools, while interpreting and communicating the improvement objectives in order to manage any resistance to change; and enhancing the collaborative exchange between schools, by facilitating the sharing of best practices, helping them to support each other, share learning, and standardise practices.

As far as Stockborough is concerned, we have explained that local authority staff did not play a role in the development of the network. Indeed, our efforts to encourage the school partners to involve them were largely rejected. Our experience elsewhere, however, has been more encouraging. This suggests that local authority staff can have an important role to play, not least in acting as the conscience of the system – making sure that all children and young people are getting a fair deal within an increasingly diverse system of education. In order to do this, they need to know the big picture about what is happening in their communities, identifying priorities for action and brokering collaboration.

All of this requires significant structural and cultural change, with local authorities moving away from a command and control perspective, towards one of enabling and facilitating collaborative action. We have experienced situations where local authority colleagues have found these changes challenging, particularly during a time of reducing budgets. Nevertheless, we remain committed to the view that local coordination – the presence of an effective 'mediating layer' – is vital.

Rethinking the role of research

What, then, does this imply for the role of research (and researchers) in relation to the development of more equitable education systems? There are, we believe, some important lessons to be drawn from our experience within this and our earlier network-based projects, although some of these are uncomfortable. Members of our team were sometimes faced with tactical dilemmas in their relationships with their school partners between their roles as observers and as participants in action. Indeed, on some occasions we were tempted to think that the stance of traditional researchers might have been safer and more comfortable. Nevertheless, we remain convinced that by attempting to create a common agenda with the schools we were able to gain greater insights into possible avenues for the development of thinking and practice.

As we explained in Chapter 2, there is currently much debate about the relationship between education research, policy-making and practice. This invites the question, of course, as to whether the fault lies with self-indulgent researchers confined to their ivory towers, or with short-sighted policy-makers and practitioners unwilling to accept any evidence which does not accord with their assumptions and immediate experiences. More importantly, it requires us to consider whether the provision of evidence for policy and practice is a proper role for research and, if not, precisely what it is that research is supposed to achieve.

Our work enables us to make an important contribution to this debate. As the accounts in this book show, we have learnt much about the difficulties that can occur as researchers attempt to negotiate appropriate working relationships with practitioners. This led us to conclude that the major omission in our earlier work was a failure to think through the nature of the knowledge each possessed, and the ways in which such knowledge might be shared and used by each group (Ainscow, Booth and Dyson, 2006b). This matter was particularly confused given that we encouraged practitioners to undertake their own research, while we as researchers involved ourselves in discussions about the detail of practice and policy.

However, within the Stockborough project, the development and research approach we explained in Chapter 2 seems to us to have been helpful in clarifying these issues. The approach does not differentiate between research-based and practice-based knowledge, much less between researcher and practitioner knowledge. It does, however, differentiate between the sorts of 'understandings' that sustain ongoing practice (and in this we include the practice of policy-making) and the 'interruptions' that can disturb such understandings. We have demonstrated how data can serve this function and that research processes can create the capacity for practitioners to step outside their current understandings.

This has implications for the relationship between researchers, policy-makers and practitioners. The critical relationship of their different kinds of knowledge has to be embodied in real encounters between these groups. This may involve close engagement, as in our network, or it may involve more distant encounters. In either event, we need new forms of relationship between practitioners and researchers, in the way that is outlined by Hiebert, Gallimore and Stigler (2002). As we explained in Chapter 2, they suggest that fruitful forms of collaboration require a reorientation of values and goals amongst both groups. Our own experience suggests that successful practitioner/researcher partnerships involve a complex social process within which colleagues with very different experiences, beliefs and methodological assumptions learn how to live with one another's differences and, even more difficult, learn how to learn from these differences.

This is why it is important to be clear that the members of our team both conducted research and were the subjects of research, as their thinking and practices were examined by themselves and others. As we engaged with data about the work of practitioners in a different context, we too were constantly challenged to think through our own practice as researchers. In the network, many teachers themselves engaged in inquiries just as academics had to struggle with the meaning of their findings for practice and had to interrogate their own assumptions in the light of practitioners' sometimes very different understandings.

In other words, the way forward for developing the relationship between research, policy-making and practice may not lie solely in engineering encounters between different groups of professionals – useful as this may be in certain cases. Rather, it requires a broadening of the repertoire of knowledge-generating strategies to which professional groups have access. In terms of what this means for teachers, all we have said about the sorts of conditions and processes for development in and between schools, and between schools and the wider community, is likely to be relevant to this expansion of repertoires.

Some final thoughts

As we finalised the text of this book, the fifth annual conference of SERN took place. As in previous years, the main event was a series of presentations by the staff inquiry groups. These were all splendid, not least in the way that they provided further confirmation of the capacity of those within schools to formulate and carry out investigations into aspects of policy and practice. It was also encouraging to hear about the way the teams had attempted to work at a whole-school level, using their findings to address challenges within their communities.

The presentations provided further insights into the nature of the challenges currently facing schools. We heard from one, for example, about the way the annual struggle to find suitable post-16 provision left some young people feeling isolated and anxious, right up to the moment the courses start; many of the schools had focused on concerns about the under-performance of particular groups; and for one, the low level of involvement in extracurricular activities amongst some groups was another focus. Interestingly, many of the groups made reference to 'invisible' students, a phrase that had emerged from the work of one school during the first year of SERN.

During the discussions following on from the presentations, concern was expressed as to whether the network could continue, partly because of the new financial pressures that exist in schools. In some schools, new factors were adding to the sense of uncertainty, with one facing closure and many others in the midst of converting into academies. Mention was made of the fact that the Association of Secondary Head Teachers had stopped meeting – possibly because of the sense of competition being created by the increased emphasis on school autonomy. We also heard worrying stories of two head teachers who had recently been absent from school as a result of what were said to be stress-related illnesses.

All of this led many of the teachers at the conference to express concerns that the state education system was in danger of fragmenting in a way that will further disadvantage some groups of young people. In particular, their concern was that with more schools becoming academies, and with the possibility of free schools being opened locally, the sense of togetherness through being part of a local authority would disappear. This led them to argue that the existence of networks within which colleagues from different schools could support one another in minimising the impact of these worrying trends was even more important. They also saw this as a means of providing an effective form of professional development at a time when practitioners are facing uncertainty about their abilities to cope with increasing pressures.

We agree with this analysis and believe that the lessons we have drawn from our experiences in Stockborough offer some helpful pointers as to the actions that are needed in order to minimise the dangers that are associated with the new policy context. Linking these lessons to our work elsewhere, we have outlined our thoughts as to how the tasks involved in developing more equitable education systems should be rethought. And, as we have explained, this requires changes at every level of the system.

The increasing focus on equity amongst policy-makers in many countries leads us to be optimistic that the time may be right to put these radical suggestions into action. In our own country, for example, the Secretary of State for Education recently stated that, '*Schools should be engines of social mobility – the places where accidents of birth and the unfairness of life's lottery are overcome through the democratisation of access to knowledge*'. This implies that we can anticipate a new wave of efforts to address the challenge of equity within the English education system. Indeed, this has already been signalled in a recent White Paper (DfE, 2010) which states that the aim '*should be to create a school system which is more effectively self-improving*'. It also argues that it will be necessary to '*design the system in a way which allows the most effective practice to spread more quickly and the best schools and leaders to take greater responsibility and extend their reach*' (p. 73).

Policy moves such as this offer new possibilities for practitioners and academic researchers to collaborate in addressing the equity agenda. This being the case, we hope that the suggestions made in this book will serve both as an inspiration and a source of helpful practical advice.

References

Ainscow, M. (1999) *Understanding the Development of Inclusive Schools.* London: Falmer.

Ainscow, M. (2005) Developing inclusive education systems: what are the levers for change? *Journal of Educational Change* 6 (2), 109–124.

Ainscow, M. (2006) 'From special education to effective schools for all: a review of progress so far'. In Florian, L. (ed.) *The Handbook of Special Education.* London: Sage.

Ainscow, M. (2010) Achieving excellence and equity: reflections on the development of practices in one local district over 10 years. *School Effectiveness and School Improvement* 21 (1), 75–91.

Ainscow, M. (2012) Moving knowledge around: strategies for fostering equity within educational systems. Journal of Educational Change (in press).

Ainscow, M. and Kaplan, I. (2005) 'Using evidence to encourage inclusive school development: possibilities and challenges'. *Australasian Journal of Special Education* 29 (2), 12–21.

Ainscow, M. and Southworth, G. (1996) School improvement: a study of the roles of leaders and external consultants. *School Effectiveness and School Improvement* 7 (3), 229–251.

Ainscow, M. and West, M. (eds) (2006) *Improving Urban Schools: Leadership and Collaboration.* Maidenhead: Open University Press (various chapters).

Ainscow, M., Booth, T. and Dyson, A. (2004) Understanding and developing inclusive practices in schools: a collaborative action research network. *International Journal of Inclusive Education* 8 (2), 125–139.

Ainscow, M., Booth, T. and Dyson, A. (2006a) Inclusion and the standards agenda: negotiating policy pressures in England. *International Journal of Inclusive Education* 10 (4–5), 295–308.

Ainscow, M., Booth, T. and Dyson, A. with Farrell, P., Frankham, J., Gallannaugh, F., Howes, A. and Smith, R. (2006b) *Improving Schools, Developing Inclusion.* London: Routledge.

Ainscow, M., Crow, M., Dyson, A., Goldrick, S., Kerr, K., Lennie, C. et al. (2006) *Equity in Education: New Directions: The Second Annual Report of the Centre for Equity in Education, University of Manchester.* Manchester: Centre for Equity in Education.

Ainscow, M., Dyson, A., Goldrick, S. and Kerr, K. (2009) 'Using research to foster equity and inclusion within the context of New Labour educational reforms'. In Chapman, C. and Gunter, G.M. (eds) *Radical Reforms: Perspectives on an Era of Educational Change.* London: Routledge.

Ainscow, M., Muijs, D. and West, M. (2006) Collaboration as a strategy for improving schools in challenging circumstances. *Improving Schools* 9 (3), 1–11.

Ainscow, M., Nicolaidou, M. and West, M. (2003) Supporting schools in difficulties: The role of school-to-school cooperation. *NFER Topic* 30, 1–4.

Ainscow, M., West, M. and Nicolaidou, M. (2005) 'Putting our heads together: a study of headteacher collaboration as a strategy for school improvement'. In Clarke, C. (ed.)*Improving Schools in Difficult Circumstances.* London: Continuum.

Anyon, J. (1997) *Ghetto Schooling: A Political Economy of Urban Educational Reform.* New York: Teachers College.

Argyris, C. and Schon, D. (1978) *Organisational Learning: A Theory of Action Perspective.* Reading MA: Addision Wesley.

Armstrong, F. and Moore, M. (2004) *Action Research for Inclusive Education: Changing Places, Changing Practices, Changing Minds.* London: Routledge.

Artiles, A. and Dyson, A. (2005) 'Inclusion, education and culture in developed and developing countries'. In Mitchell, D. (ed.)*Contextualising Inclusive Education: Evaluating Old and New International Perspectives.* London: Routledge.

Ball, S. J. (2003) The teacher's soul and the terrors of performativity. *Journal of Education Policy* 18 (2), 215–228.

Ball, S. J. (2008) *The Education Debate.* Bristol: The Policy Press.

Ball, S. J. (2010) New class inequalities in education. *International Journal of Sociology and Social Policy* 30 (3/4), 155–166.

Beveridge, S. W. (1942) Social Insurance and Allied Services. London: HMSO.

Blair, T. (2005) *Higher Standards: Better Schools. Speech on Education at 10 Downing Street 24 October 2005.* Available online at: http://www.pm.gov.uk/output/Page8363.asp (accessed 8 September 2011).

Blunkett, D. (1999) *Excellence for the Many, Not Just the Few: Raising Standards and Extending Opportunities in Our Schools. The CBI President's Reception Address by the Rt. Hon. David Blunkett MP 19 July 1999.* London: DfEE.

Booth, T. and Ainscow, M. (2002) *Index for Inclusion: Developing Learning and Participation in Schools* (2nd edn). Bristol: Centre for Studies on Inclusive Education.

Braveman, P. (2003) Monitoring equity in health and healthcare: a conceptual framework. *Journal of Health, Population and Nutrition* 21 (3), 181–192.

Brighouse, T. (2007) The London Challenge – a personal view. In Brighouse, T. and Fullick, L. (eds) *Education in a Global City.* London: Institute of Education Bedford Way Papers.

Broadfoot, P. (2001) 'Empowerment or performativity? Assessment policy in the late twentieth century'. In Phillips, R. and Furlong, J. (eds) *Education, Reform and the State: Twenty-Five Years of Politics, Policy and Practice.* London: RoutledgeFalmer.

Cameron, D. (2011) *PM's speech at Munich security conference.* London: The Prime Minister's Office. Available online at: http://www.number10.gov.uk/news/speeches-and-transcripts/2011/02/pms-speech-at-munich-security-conference-60293 (accessed 24 June 2011).

Cantle, T. C. (2001) *Community Cohesion: A Report of the Independent Review Team*. Report for Home Office (London).

Carr, W. and Kemmis, S. (1986) *Becoming Critical: Education, Knowledge and Action Research*. London: Falmer Press.

Chapman, C., Ainscow, M. Bragg, J., Gallannaugh, F., Mongon, D., Muijs, D. et al. (2008) *New Models of Leadership: Reflections on ECM Policy, Leadership and Practice*. Nottingham: NCSL.

Chapman, C., Lindsay, G., Muijs, D. and Harris, A. (2010) The federations policy: from partnership to integration for school improvement? *School Effectiveness and Improvement* 21 (1), 53–74.

Chapman, C. and Gunter, H. (eds) (2009) *Radical Reforms: Perspectives on an Era of Educational Change*. London: Routledge.

Checkland, P. (1981) *Systems Thinking, Systems Practice*. Chichester: Wiley.

Checkland, P. and Scholes, J. (1990) *Soft Systems Methodology in Action*. Chichester: Wiley.

Chenoweth, K., (2007) *It's Being Done: Academic Success in Unexpected Schools*. Cambridge, MA: Harvard Education Press.

Clark, C., Dyson, A., Millward, A. and Robson, S. (1999) Theories of inclusion, theories of schools: deconstructing and reconstructing the 'inclusive school'. *British Educational Research Journal* 25 (2), 157–177.

Clarke, P., Ainscow, M. and West, M. (2005) 'Learning from difference: some reflections on school improvement projects in three countries'. In Harris, A. (ed.) *International Developments in School Improvement*. London: Continuum.

Cobb, P., Confrey, J., diSessa, A., Lehrer, R., and Schauble, L. (2003) Design experiments in educational research. *Educational Researcher* 32 (1 Jan/Feb), 9–13.

Collins, J. (2001) *From Good to Great*. New York: William Collins.

Crowther, D., Cummings, C., Dyson, A. and Millward, A. (2003) *Schools and Area Regeneration*. Bristol: The Policy Press.

Cummings, C., Dyson, A. and Todd, L. (2011) *Beyond the School Gate: Can Full Service and Extended Schools Overcome Disadvantage?* London: Routledge.

DCSF (2008) *21st Century Schools: A World Class Education for Every Child*. London: DCSF Publications.

DCSF IDeA and LGA (2007) Narrowing the gap in outcomes. Available online at: http://www.lga.gov.uk/lga/aio/21949 (accessed 14 June 2010).

Department for Education (2010) *The Schools White Paper: the Importance of Teaching*. London: DfE.

Design-Based Research Collective (2003) Design-based research: an emerging paradigm for educational inquiry. *Educational Researcher* 32 (1), 5–8.

DfES (2001a) *Inclusive schooling: Children with special educational needs. Ref dfes/0774/2001*. London: DfES.

DfES (2001b) *The National Literacy and Numeracy Strategies Intervention Programmes*. London: DfES.

DfES (2003) *Every Child Matters. Cm. 5860*. London: The Stationery Office.

DfES (2005) *Ethnicity and Education: The Evidence on Minority Ethnic Pupils. Research Topic Paper 01-05*. Report for DfES (London).

Dobbie, W. and Fryer, R. G. (2009) *Are High-Quality Schools Enough to Close the Achievement Gap? Evidence from a Bold Social Experiment in Harlem.* Cambridge: Harvard University.

Dyson, A. and Millward, A. (2000) *Schools and Special Needs: Issues of Innovation and Inclusion.* London: Paul Chapman.

Dyson, A. and Raffo, C. (2007) Education and disadvantage: the role of community-orientated schools. *Oxford Review of Education* 33 (3), 297–314.

Dyson, A., Gallannaugh, F. and Millward, A. (2003) Making space in the standards agenda: developing inclusive practices in schools. *European Educational Research Journal* 2 (2), 228–244.

Ebbutt, D. (1985) 'Educational action research: some general concerns and specific quibbles'. In Burgess, G. (ed.) *Issues in Educational Research: Qualitative Methods.* London: Falmer Press.

Elliott, J. (1991) *Action Research for Educational Change.* Milton Keynes: Open University Press.

Equality and Human Rights Commission (2010) *How Fair is Britain? Equality, Human Rights and Good Relations in 2010. The First Triennial Review.* Report for Equality and Human Rights Commission (London).

Eraut, M. (1994) *Developing Professional Knowledge and Competence.* London: Falmer Press.

Fielding, M. (2004) Transformative approaches to student voice: theoretical underpinnings, recalcitrant realites. *BERJ* 30 (2), 295–311.

Fraser, N. (2008) *Scales of Justice: Reimagining Political Space in a Globalizing World.* Cambridge: Polity Press.

Fryer, R. and Levitt, S. (2004) Understanding the black-white test score gap in the first two years of school. *The Review of Economics and Statistics*, 86 (2), 447–464.

Fukuda-Parr, S. (2003) The human development paradigm: operationalising Sen's ideas on capabilities. *Feminist Economics* 9 (2–3), 301–317.

Gillborn, D. and Mirza, H. S. (2000) *Educational Inequality: Mapping Race, Class and Gender. A Synthesis of Research Evidence for the Office for Standards in Education.* London: Ofsted.

Giroux, H. A. and Schmidt, M. (2004) Closing the achievement gap: a metaphor for children left behind. *Journal of Educational Change* 5 (3), 213–228.

Goodman, A., Sibieta, L. and Elizabeth, W. (2009) *Inequalities in Educational Outcomes Among Children Aged 3 to 16: Final Report for the National Equality Panel, September 2009.* Report for national equalities Panel, Government Equalities Office (London).

Gray, J. (2010) 'Probing the limits of systemic reform: the English case'. In Hargreaves, A., Lieberman, A., Fullan, M. and Hopkins D. (eds) *Second International Handbook of Educational Change.* Dordrecht: Springer.

Gunter, H. M. (ed.) (2011) *The State and Education Policy: The Academies Programme.* London: Continuum.

Handy, C. B. (1991) *Understanding Organisations* (rev. edn). Harmondsworth: Penguin Books.

Hargreaves, D. H. (1995) School culture, school effectiveness and school improvement. *School Effectiveness and School Improvement* 6 (1), 23–46.

Hargreaves, D. H. (1999) The knowledge creating school. *British Journal of Educational Studies* 42 (2), 122–144.

Hargreaves, D. H. (2010) *Creating a Self-Improving School System*. Nottingham: National College for Leadership of Schools and Children's services.

Hiebert, J., Gallimore, R. and Stigler, J. W. (2002) A knowledge base for the teaching profession: what would it look like and how can we get one? *Educational Researcher* 31 (5), 3–15.

Hillage, J., Pearson, R., Anderson, A. and Tamkin, P. (1998) Excellence in Research on Schools. DfEE Research Report RR74. London: DfEE.

Hopkins, D. (2007) *Every School a Great School: Realizing the Potential of System Leadership*. Maidenhead: Open University Press.

Hopkins, D., Ainscow, M. and West, M. (1994) *School Improvement in an Era of Change*. London: Cassell.

Hopkins, D., Reynolds, D. and Gray, J. (2005) *School Improvement: Lessons from Research*. London: DfES.

Hopkins, D., West, M. and Ainscow, M. (1996) *Improving the Quality of Education for All: Progress and Challenge*. London: David Fulton.

House, E. R. (1979) 'Technology versus craft: a ten year perspective on educational innovation'. In Tayor, P.H. (ed.) *New Directions in Curriculum Studies*. Lewes: Falmer Press.

Howes, A., and Ainscow, M. (2006). 'Collaboration with a city-wide purpose: Making paths for sustainable educational improvement'. In Ainscow, M. and West, M. (eds.)*Improving Urban School: Leadership and Collaboration*. Maidenhead: Open University Press, 104–116.

Howes, A., Booth, T., Dyson, A. and Frankham, J. (2005) Teacher learning and the development of inclusive practices and policies: framing and context. *Research Papers in Education* 20 (2), 131–146.

Howes, A., Frankham J., Ainscow, M. and Farrell, P. (2004) The action in action research: mediating and developing inclusive intentions. *Educational Action Research* 12 (2), 239–257.

Johnston, R., Burgess, S., Harris, R. and Wilson, D. (2006) '*Sleep-Walking Towards Segregation?*' The Changing Ethnic Composition of English Schools, 1997–2003: An Entry Cohort Analysis. Working Paper No. 06/155. Report for Centre for Market and Public Organisation, University of Bristol (Bristol).

Kelly, R. (2005) Education and social progress. 26 july 2005. Available online at: http://www.dfes.gov.uk/speeches/speech.cfm?SpeechID=242 (accessed 4 August 2005).

Kemmis, S. and McTaggart, R. (1988) *The Action Research Planner* (3rd edn). Victoria: Deakin University Press.

Kerr, K. and West, M. (eds) (2010) *Insight 2: Social Inequality: Can Schools Narrow the Gap?* Macclesfield: British Education Research Association.

Le Metais, J. (1997) Values and aims in curriculum and assessment frameworks. Available online at: http://www.inca.org.uk/pdf/values_no_intro_97.pdf.

Levin, B. (2005) Thinking about improvements in schools in challenging circumstances. Paper presented at the American Educational Research Association, Montreal, April.

Lewin, K. (1946) Action research and minority problems. *Journal of Social Issues* 2, 34–36.

Lima, J. A. (2008) Thinking more deeply about networks in education. *Journal of Educational Change* 11 (1), 1–21.

Lipman, P. (2004) *High Stakes Education: Inequality, Globalisation and Urban School Reform.* New York: Routledge.

Lo, M. L., Yan, P. W., and Pakey, C. P. M. (eds) (2005) *For Each and Everyone: Catering for Individual Differences through Learning Studies.* Hong Kong: Hong Kong University Press.

Lupton, R. (2006) *How Does Place Affect Education?* London: IPPR.

Macpherson, I., Aspland, T., Elliot, B., Proudfoot, C., Shaw, L. and Thurlow, G. (1998) 'A journey into learning partnership: a university and state system working together for curriculum change'. In Atweh, B., Kemmis, S. and Weeks, P. (eds) *Action Research in Practice.* London: Routledge.

McIntyre, D. (2005) Bridging the gap between research and practice. *Cambridge Journal of Education* 35 (3), 357–382.

Meyland-Smith, D. and Evans, N. (2009) *A Guide to School Choice Reforms.* London: Policy Exchange.

Miles, S. and Ainscow, M. (2011) *Responding to Diversity in Schools: An Inquiry Based Approach.* London: Routledge.

Mourshed, M., Chijioke, C. and Barber, M. (2010) *How the World's Most Improved School Systems Keep Getting Better.* McKinsey and Company.

Muijs, D., Ainscow, M., Chapman, C. and West, M. (2011) *Collaboration and Networking in Education.* London: Springer.

Muijs, D., West, M. and Ainscow, M. (2010) Why network? Theoretical perspectives on networking. *School Effectiveness and School Improvement* 21 (1), 5–26.

Mulford, B. (2007) 'Building social capital in professional learning communities: Importance, challenges and a way forward'. In Stoll, L. and Seashore Louis, K. (eds)*Professional Learning Communities: Divergence, Depth and Dilemmas.* London: Open University Press.

National Education Research Forum (2000) *Research and Development for Education.* Nottingham: NERF Publications.

National Education Research Forum (2001) *A Research and Development Strategy for Education: Developing Quality and Diversity.* Nottingham: NERF Publications.

Nonaka, I. and Takeuchi, H. (1995) *The Knowledge Creating Company.* Oxford: OUP.

OECD (2007) *No More Failures: Ten Steps to Equity in Education.* Paris: OECD.

OECD (2010), *PISA 2009 Results: Overcoming Social Background – Equity in Learning Opportunities and Outcomes* (Vol. II). Paris: OECD.

O'Hanlon, C. (2003) *Educational Inclusion as Action Research: An Interpretive Discourse.* Maidenhead: Open University Press.

Oja, S. N. and Smulyan, L. (1989) *Collaborative Action Research: A Developmental Approach.* London: Falmer Press.

Payne, C. M. (2008) *So Much Reform, So Little Change: The Persistence of Failure in Urban Schools.* Cambridge: Harvard Education Press.

Phillips, M., Crouse, J. and Ralph, J. (1998) 'Does the black-white test score gap widen after children enter school?' In Jencks, C. and Phillips, M. (eds)*The Black-White Test Score Gap.* Washington, DC: The Brookings Institute.

Primary Review (2007) How well are we doing? Research on standards, quality and assessment in English primary education. Available online at: http://www.prima-ryreview.org.uk/Downloads/Int_Reps/2.Standards_quality_assessment/Primary_Review_Standards-quality-assessment_overview_briefing_071102.pdf (accessed 12 March 2008).

Putnam, R. D. (2000) *Bowling Alone*. New York: Simon and Schuster.

Rosenholtz, S. (1989) *Teachers' Workplace: The Social Organisation of Schools*. New York: Longman.

Sammons, P. (2007) *School Effectiveness and Equity: Making Connections*. Reading: CfBT.

Schein, E. (1985) *Organisational Culture and Leadership*. San Francisco: Jossey-Bass.

Schools Analysis and Research Division, D. F. C. S. A. F. (2009) *Deprivation and education: The Evidence on Pupils in England, Foundation Stage to Key Stage 4*. Report for DCSF (London).

Sen, A. (1980) 'Equality of what?' In McMurrin, S. (ed.) *The Tanner Lectures on Human Values* (Vol. 1). Cambridge: Cambridge University Press.

Sen, A. (2000) *Social Exclusion: Concept, Application, and Scrutiny*. Social Development Papers No. 1, Office of Environment and Social Development, Asian Development Bank, June 2000.

Sen, A. (2009) *The Idea of Justice*. London: Allen Lane.

Senge, P. M. (1989) The Fifth Discipline: The Art and Practice of the Learning Organisation. London: Century.

Social Exclusion Unit (2001) *Preventing Social Exclusion*. Report for Social Exclusion Unit (London).

Stringfield, S. (1995) Attempting to Improve Students' Learning through Innovative Programs – The Case for Schools Evolving into High Reliability Organizations. *School Effectiveness and School Improvement* 6 (1), 67–96.

Sutton Trust (2005) *Rates of Eligibility for Free School Meals at the Top State Schools*. Report for The Sutton Trust. Available online at: http://www.suttontrust.com/research/rates-of-eligibility-for-fsm-at-the-top-state-schools/ (accessed 8 September 2011).

Thrupp, M. and Lupton, R. (2006) Taking school contexts more seriously: the social justice challenge. *British Journal of Educational Studies* 54, 308–328.

UNESCO (2010) *EFA Global Monitoring Report: Reaching the Marginalized*. Paris: UNESCO/Oxford University Press.

Wenger, E. (1999) *Communities of Practice: Learning, Meaning and Identity*. Cambridge: Cambridge University Press.

West, A., Barham, E. and Hind, A. (2009) *Secondary School Admissions in England: Policy and Practice*. London: Report for London School of Economics and Political Science.

West, M. (1998) 'Working with the grain – creating a sustainable improvement model for the self-managing school'. In Fullan, M. (ed.) *International Handbook of Educational Change*. Dordecht/Boston/London: Kluwer Academic Publishers.

West, M. (2000) Supporting School Improvement: observations on the inside, reflections from the outside. *School Leadership and Management* 20 (1), 43–60.

West, M. and Ainscow, M. (2010) 'Improving schools in Hong Kong: a description of the improvement model and some reflections on its impact on schools, teachers and school principals'. In Huber, S. (ed.), *School Leadership – International Perspectives*. London: Springer.

West, M., Ainscow, M. and Stanford, J. (2005) Sustaining improvement in schools in challenging circumstances: a study of successful practice. *School Leadership and Management* 25 (1), 77–93.

Whitehurst, G. J. and Croft. M. (2010) *The Harlem Children's Zone, Promise Neighborhoods, and the Broader, Bolder Approach to Education*. Washington: The Brookings Institution.

Whitty, G. (2010) 'Marketization and post-marketization in education'. In Hargreaves, A., Lieberman, A., Fullan, M. and Hopkins, D. (eds) *Second International Handbook of Educational Change*. Dordrecht: Springer.

Wilkinson, R. and Pickett, K. (2000) *The Spirit Level*. London: Allen Lane.

Index

academic progress 80–2, 81*f*
academies 12, 164
access 35, 123–4
accountability 154
action research 18–19; critical
   collaborative action research 25–30
advanced skills teachers (AST) 68, 96,
   97, 98, 99
assessment systems 13, 125
attendance problems 88
attitudes and practices 122–3

Ball, S. J. 151–2
between-school collaboration 26–7,
   28–9, 107, 108–9, 113–16, 154–7, 160
between-school equity 6, 114, 142, 155
Beveridge, S. W. 9
beyond-school equity 6, 139–41, 142,
   143–5, 151–3, 157–9, 160
Blair, T. 27, 138
Blunkett, D. 12
Braveman, P. 34
bullying 71–2, 79

capabilities 7–8, 35
Castle High 46*t*, 56, 105–6, 113
Central High 46*t*, 74; cultural
   change 144; inquiry team 95–6;
   networking 114; observation 89;
   post-16 education 140–1;
   student performance 39*t*;
   underachievement 43*t*
children's services 144, 147
collaboration: equity-focused
   local leadership 145–6; local
   coordination 124–5, 154, 161–2;
   researchers and practitioners 22,

33, 163; between schools 26–7,
   28–9, 107, 108–9, 113–16, 154–7, 160;
   within schools 104; whole-system
   approach 145, 160
Collins, J. 99
community: analysing community
   contexts 24–5; involving the school
   community 52; wider community
   development 143–4, 146, 160
conditions for fostering equity 145–7,
   149–50
context analysis 24–5, 50, 157–9, 159*t*
critical friends 26, 27, 30, 31, 46, 56, 108,
   119–20, 157
cultural capital 136
cultural change 86, 99–110;
   adjustment 102–6; collective
   culture 108–9; leadership 106–7, 114;
   ownership 109–10; resistance 100–2;
   role of university team 109–10
curriculum content 124–5

data: reviewing existing data 87–8;
   generating questions 88–9; gathering
   additional data 89–91; involving
   students directly 91–4; making sense
   of the data 94
decision-making 8
Department for Education 165
design-based research 18
development and research 20, 163;
   framework 31–3; knowledge-
   generation 33, 164; relationships 33
dialogical imperative 118
differences of practice 24
distribution 7, 8, 11
Dobbie, W. 152

EAL *see* English as an additional language
East Town High 46*t*
ecology of equity 16, 141–8; beyond
    schools 142, 143–5, 151–3; conditions
    for fostering equity 145–7; between
    schools 142; within schools 141,
    142–3
education policy 165; accountability 154;
    in England 11–14, 58–9, 151–2, 153,
    165; equity as policy goal 112–13; and
    local actions 146–7, 154; rethinking
    policy 152–4; sense of purpose 153;
    stakeholders 153
educational action research 18–19
engagement 19
English as an additional language
    (EAL) 67, 68, 70–4, 72*f*, 73*f*, 139–40,
    156
environment 10, 15, 151
equitable schools 122–6; access 123–4;
    assessment systems 125; attitudes
    and practices 122–3; curriculum
    content 124–5
equity in education 1–16; case
    histories 2–5; common sense of
    purpose 153; defining equity 2–5,
    34–5; England 8–14; frameworks
    for understanding 5–8; as policy
    goal 112–13; rethinking equity
    in education 150–2; school-
    focused approaches 151; school
    perspective 14–15
equity indicators 114, 115, 115*t*
equity research network *see* Stockborough
    Equity Research Network (SERN)
ethics 90
ethnicity 9–10, 11, 45, 67, 74–5, 95, 130,
    140
Every Child Matters (2003) 14
evidence: collecting evidence 50–1;
    making sense of the evidence 51
excellence 12, 13, 14
external partners 52–3
extracurricular activities 76–82, 78*f*; and
    academic progress 80–2, 81*f*

'failing' schools 12, 15
fairness 2, 34–5, 93, 147, 150
faith schools 10
Families of Schools 156
Fielding, M. 118
frameworks for understanding

equity 5–8; capability 7–8; decision-
    making 8; distribution, recognition
    and representation 7, 8, 11, 14; root
    causes 6; values 8
Fraser, N. 7
Fryer, R. G. 151, 152

gender 9–10
Giroux, H. A. 18
Greater Manchester Challenge 155–7
Greenside Grammar 46*t*, 122

Handy, C. B. 107, 120
Hanley, L. 136
Hargreaves, D. H. 160
Harlem Children's Zone 152
head teachers 59, 106–7, 114, 137, 140,
    143–4, 164
Hiebert, J. *et al.* 33, 163
Highlands High 46*t*; cultural
    resistance 100–1; leadership 107;
    local environment 38; new
    arrivals 43*t*, 67–74, 135, 139,
    142; student performance 39*t*;
    vulnerability 45, 139–40, 143
House, E. R. 85
hub schools 156

impact of project on schools 111–16;
    educational equity as policy goal
    112–13; increased networking
    activity 113–16; policy into practice 113;
    student performance 112; *see also* staff
    development
Improving the Quality of Education for All
    (IQEA) 20–5; collaboration 22;
    contract 21–2; features 21;
    framework 22–3, 23*f*; inquiry-based
    approaches 23–5; principles 20–1
inclusion 10–11, 35, 150; *see also*
    Understanding and Developing Inclusive
    Practices in Schools
inquiry-based approaches 23–5
inquiry teams 40–1, 119–22;
    empowerment 119; role of
    university team 109–10; school as
    unit of analysis 127–8; stages of
    development 120–2, 121*t*; status of
    teams 95–7; *see also* networking

Keys to Success 156
knowledge-generation 33, 164

Le Metais, J. 118
leadership: analysing leadership 24;
    and community 143–4; equity-
    focused local leadership 145–6; and
    organisational culture 106–7, 114
Leafy Top High 46*t*, 90, 112–13
learner experiences 24
learning communities 143–4
learning organisations 122, 154, 160
learning walks 90
lesson study 23–4, 58
Levitt, S. 151
Lima, J. A. 160
literacy 13, 76
local authorities: role 154, 161–2;
    Stockborough 38, 40–1, 46, 55, 58,
    130, 132, 135, 143, 145–6
Long Road Church of England High 46*t*,
    139; invisible students 87–8, 90–1;
    student–staff relationships 101–2

Macpherson, I. *et al.* 25
McKinsey report 150–1, 161
monitoring progress 53
Moorside High 46*t*, 128, 129–39;
    attendance 43*t*, 88; cultural
    adjustment 104; endgame
    133–6; inquiry team 96–7;
    leadership 107; limits of within-
    school approaches 136–9; local
    environment 38, 129, 143–4; social
    and educational divisions 129–31, 142;
    Special Measures 39, 45, 56, 133–5;
    student performance 39*t*; troubled
    past 131–3; wider implications
    139–41; workshops 91
Mourshed, M. *et al.* 150–1, 161
moving schools 122
Mulford, B. 160
multiculturism 11

National Challenge 46
National Curriculum 124
National Education Research Forum
    (NERF) 18
national literacy strategies 13
national numeracy strategies 13
networking 48, 49, 54, 57, 104, 113–16,
    120, 160

observations 28, 29, 43–4, 47, 63–5, 71,
    89–90, 102, 103

OECD (Organisation for Economic Co-
    operation and Development) 34–5,
    150, 151
Ofsted (Office for Standards in
    Education) 12, 132–3, 134, 137
opportunities 10
Our Lady's Roman Catholic High 46*t*,
    89–90, 124, 135
out-of-school-hours (OOSH)
    activities 76–82, 78*f*; and academic
    progress 80–2, 81*f*
outcomes 9–10, 13, 35
Outwood High 46*t*, 144

participation 35
Payne, C. M. 159–60
peer pressure 79–80
performativity 12–13, 14–15
Phillips, M. *et al.* 151
planning framework 50*f*; analysis of
    context 50; collecting evidence 50–1;
    involving external partners 52–3;
    making sense of the evidence 51;
    monitoring progress 53; moving
    forward, involving others 52
political processes 86, 94–9; changing
    membership 97–9; school teams 95–7
post-16 education 140–1, 164
power 19–20
Putnam, R. D. 159

recognition 7, 11, 14
relationships: researchers and
    practitioners 22, 33, 53–4, 109–10,
    163–4; social capital 159–61; student–
    staff relationships 101–2, 103–4
representation 7, 11
researching equity 17–36; common
    strands 30–1; design-based
    research 18; development and
    research 20, 31–3, 163, 164;
    educational action research
    18–19; engagement 19; inclusion
    network 25–30; power 19–20;
    research and development 18, 19;
    role of research 53–4, 109–10, 162–4;
    school improvement project 20–5;
    transfer 20; values 19–20, 33–5
Rosenholtz, S. 122

Schein, E. 106
Schmidt, M. 18

school as unit of analysis 127–8; wider
implications 139–41; *see also* Moorside
High
school change 85–110; cultural view 86,
99–110; political view 86, 94–9;
technical view 85, 86–94
school improvement project 20–5
school selection 10, 12
school transitions 67–74, 135–6, 137,
138
segregation 11
Sen, A. 7, 35
Senge, P. M. 122
SERN *see* Stockborough Equity Research
Network
SERN model 48–54; actions 49;
planning framework 50–3, 50*f*;
propositions 49; university team
support 53–4, 109–10
social capital 56, 136, 159–61
social disadvantage 35, 45, 124, 136,
137
social exclusion 13
socio-economic status 9, 10, 17–18, 123,
138, 159
South Dale High 46*t*, 135, 140, 143;
out-of-school-hours (OOSH)
activities 76–82, 78*f*, 81*f*
Southside 90
special education 10–11, 13–14, 105,
156
staff culture 102
staff development 96–7, 116–19;
challenging current orthodoxy 118–
19; listening and learning 116–17;
professional growth 117–18
stakeholders 153
Stockborough Equity Research Network
(SERN) 37–60; areas of focus 42,
43*t*, 45, 61–2; building up the
network 45–8, 46*t*; conferences 55–6,
164; context 37–9, 39*t*; designing the
project 39–40; developing roles 56–7,
67, 96; equity indicators 114, 115,
115*t*; impact on schools 111–16;
organisational arrangements 54–6;
school processes 41–5; the SERN
model 48–54; setting up the
network 38; staff inquiry groups
40–1, 95–7, 119–22, 127–8; student
workshops 48, 55, 91–4; system
change 57–9

student focus groups 44, 64–5, 68–9,
71–2, 75–6, 79–80, 90, 91
student performance 13, 39*t*, 112, 124–5,
131, 133, 135, 137
student voice 45, 94, 102, 116, 118
student workshops 48, 55, 91–4
students: Asian British boys 74–6;
attendance 88; disaffected
students 74–6; English as an
additional language (EAL) 67, 68,
70–4, 72*f*, 73*f*, 139–40, 156; and
extracurricular activities 76–82, 78*f*,
81*f*; invisible students 62–7, 87–8,
90–1, 164; new arrivals 67–74, 122,
139–40; stereotypes 88
student–staff relationships 101–2,
103–4
support staff 104

targets 13
teachers: attitudes and practices 122–3;
empowerment 109, 119; equity 102;
head teachers 59, 106–7, 114,
137, 140, 143–4, 164; invisible
teachers 101–2; responsibilities 153;
staffing 123–4; support staff 104;
surveillance of 15; *see also* inquiry
teams
teaching: analysing teaching 23–4
teaching assistants 95, 96, 98–9, 105
teaching schools 156
technical processes 85, 86–94; starting
with hunches 86–7; reviewing existing
data 87–8; generating questions 88–9;
gathering additional data 89–91;
involving students directly 91–4;
making sense of the data 94
transfer 20

*Understanding and Developing Inclusive
Practices in Schools* 25–30;
action 25–6; collaboration 26–7,
28–9; critical friends 26, 27, 30, 31;
interruptions 28, 30; problems 30;
project outcomes 29–30; research 26;
school-to-school visits 28–9;
standards 27; values 27
United States 8, 18, 150–1, 152, 159–60

Valley High 38, 46*t*; cultural
adjustment 102–4; inquiry team 98;
invisible students 43*t*, 62–7, 87,

90; leadership 106–7; student
performance 39*t*; student–staff
relationships 102
values 8, 19–20, 33–5

Wenger, E. 28

West, M. 120
Westbury High 46*t*, 74–6
Westlands High 46*t*
within-school collaboration 104
within-school equity 6, 141, 142–3, 154,
160